A WORLD ON HOLD

A Living Record of the Global Pandemic

EDITED BY

DIVITA AGGARWAL - SURABHI SUNDARAM

Om Books International

First published in 2022 by

Om Books International

Corporate & Editorial Office
A-12, Sector 64, Noida 201 301
Uttar Pradesh, India
Phone: +91 120 477 4100
Email: editorial@ombooks.com
Website: www.ombooksinternational.com

Sales Office
107, Ansari Road, Darya Ganj,
New Delhi 110 002, India
Phone: +91 11 4000 9000
Fax: +91 11 2327 8091
Email: sales@ombooks.com
Website: www.ombooks.com

ISBN: 978-93-94547-07-0

Printed in India

10 9 8 7 6 5 4 3 2 1

Surabhi Sundaram is a writer and video producer with an appetite for non-fiction. Her work predominantly includes reportage of human-interest stories and current affairs through the visual as well as the written form. During the first and second waves of the Covid-19 pandemic, Surabhi was on the ground at hospitals, crematoriums, migrant worker camps and vaccination centres to understand the impact of the pandemic in India. When Surabhi isn't writing, you will most likely find her binge-watching movies or TV shows, or playing a racquet sport. Surabhi plans to write her next book around the theme of war and conflict.

Divita Aggarwal is a published author and entrepreneur. She first began creating other worlds and characters through her debut novel, at the age of sixteen. Shortly after completing her degree in economics honours from Ashoka University, Divita started working at the forefront of understanding the industrial impact of the pandemic. Apart from writing, she is deeply passionate about start-ups and has committed to independently building a venture. A professionally trained taekwondo player, she loves to read non-fiction books that lend palpable significance to relevant matters. Divita lives and works out of her home in New Delhi and spends her off-days delivering talks at public forums, experimenting with exercise and different cuisines.

This book is dedicated to all frontline workers across the world.

We express immense gratitude to you for putting humanity above all else. Thank you for your known and unknown sacrifices, for being our friends in the neediest hour, for embodying the true essence of heroism. It is your incomparable strength that made the fight against COVID-19 possible.

Contents

Acknowledgements

Exciting and frustrating – two emotions we would use to describe the process of writing and publishing this book. For young authors, there is a lot that isn't apparent at the outset: how challenging it would be to convert early scribbles into something that resembles a book, the meticulousness when conducting research, the patient road to finding the right home for your words – the list is too long. For that reason and so many more, these acknowledgements go out to everyone who helped make the process, setbacks and all, smoother. For everyone who stepped up, offered valuable feedback, those who showed support in the form of optimistic energy, those who held us accountable, and those without whom this book simply would have been eminently less readable – we are so, so grateful.

As simple as this may sound, this book is a product of a late-night conversation between two friends who, in the midst of a global pandemic, found themselves lost, helpless but curious. Curious to delve deeper into the pandemic's wide-ranging effects on people from all walks of life, to provide hope in a time when negativity blanketed the world, to showcase the many acts of bravery across the world. And, we are thankful for all those who showed the courage, open-mindedness and patience to address our curiosity. Our contributors, all twenty of them, demonstrated exceptional resilience while sharing their deepest emotions with us, and now, you. We are thankful for the authenticity in your words, the bravery in your actions and most importantly, your trust in us to do justice to your story.

Many people were extremely welcoming and helpful in the process of getting us in touch with many of our contributors. A special word for Shalvi Biswas Mangaokar and John Koshy (Chief of Staff [Delhi] to Dr Shashi Tharoor), for their belief in our idea, helping manoeuvre logistical hiccups and for offering (rather innovative) words of advice at different stages of the process.

Two individuals risked their lives during the pandemic to document the visual landscape of this period and were extremely kind to willingly share their work with us: Md. Meharban and Wasim Sarvar. Their photography provided the visual stimulation required to complete the book.

The most excitingly unsettling parts of this journey began when we put the final full-stop to the manuscript. A million question marks, tens of drafts of the pitch proposal, wondering whether or not we've set our ambition too high. To our very great fortune, we then crossed paths with our literary agent, Suhail Mathur (The Book Bakers), who came as a strong ray of hope. His belief in the idea is what turned things around. We are most thankful for his dedicated work ethic, his focus on treating this book as his own, and his willingness to deliver exactly what we aspired for.

A special vote of thanks to someone who took our early, much-too-long, far-too-redundant draft and converted it into a tightened manuscript. Shantanu Ray Chaudhuri (Editor-in-chief, Om Books International) was enormously helpful in shaping the manuscript. We are thankful for his apt sense of what works on paper and what doesn't.

Another person instrumental in the initial writing process has been a freelance editor, Ateendriya Gupta. She was not only incredibly helpful with the detailed line editing and checking of our manuscript, but also repeatedly called our attention to structural problems, statements that we really couldn't support with facts, and redundancy. Both Shantanu and Ateendriya adopted the book as their own and put extraordinary hours and matchless care into its development.

Finally, we want to acknowledge with gratitude, the love and support of our closest friends and family. Our parents, Sunjey, Ruchi, Brig. R. Sundaram, Suchitra. Our siblings, Pranav and Suditi. Our friends, Vansh, Vedika, Shreya, Bhavya, Teesta, Ayush, Srishti, Saloni, Kinjal, Varsha. All of them kept us going, and this book would not have been possible without their words of encouragement.

Lastly, thank you to those who give us purpose to write, without whom this book may never have existed – our readers. Each one of you reading this right now is valuable as you symbolize and instil the belief in our ability to tell stories.

Preface

Divita Aggarwal and Surabhi Sundaram

No one who has lived through this era will ever get over the overwhelming emotions the pandemic has engendered—the trauma and helplessness of lives upended, felt by the entirety of the world's population. For the first time in modern history, humans—rich or poor, black or white, religious or non-religious—have been unsparingly affected by the exact same situation, at the exact same time. Covid-19, a novel respiratory virus that originated in Wuhan, China, in December 2019, was declared a global pandemic by the World Health Organisation on 11 March 2020. This highly contagious and rapidly spreading virus crippled the entire world, and plunged it into a medical, economic, psychological and social crisis. Millions of small business owners declared bankruptcy, hundreds of thousands of people lost their jobs overnight and a shroud of uncertainty descended over the world. Covid-19 also came to be known as the world's first digital pandemic, predominantly in its effects. Around 3.8 billion people were accessing 24/7 updates of positive cases, death tolls, details and discoveries. Until now, no disease outbreak—Swine Flu, Ebola or SARS—had attracted such unprecedented dialogue on media or social media. Covid-19 brought with it a collective grief of incomparable proportions.

This book is a chronicle of this historic period. It is a documentation of compelling experiences of individuals living through an unprecedented global pandemic, to display how the human race as a whole struggled with a similar situation with each of us creating our very own coping mechanisms. The motivation to write this book came from an earnest need to contribute and be active participants in the fight against Covid-19. Watching frontline workers risking their lives tirelessly and people everywhere stepping up to do everything in their capacity made us ask ourselves: how could we do our bit during this difficult time? One of us is a video producer, who had to be on the field during the outbreak to identify and film stories. Spending two months reporting on the subject and visiting crematoriums, hospitals, railway stations and burial grounds, as well as meeting the affected people, fuelled our urge to tell their stories. We were looking for narratives that would become windows into the ordeals of people from different walks of life, while also serving as a ray of hope and a point of remembrance. By documenting stories of innovation and coping, we aimed to give the readers the feeling that if the twenty people whose stories have been documented here could get through it, so can they. We wanted to bring to people, all of whom are dealing with the pandemic in their own ways, a wide range of emotional and physical struggles, documented in real time.

We began by looking into the industries that were most adversely affected and found people within those industries who had compelling stories to tell. The selection process was guided by our curiosity to learn how the pandemic affected lives in different ways and how people improvised and displayed strength. In our effort to offer experiences that were relatively less known and understood—ones that would provide new perspectives to the fight against the virus—what has come together finally is a mix of gut-wrenching stories, personal accounts and informative narratives. While the omnipresence of this pandemic has connected people, these distinct experiences underline how different the recuperation process has been for everyone. By journaling their experiences in this book, we intend to keep an active record that is representative of how 7.8 billion people emerged from what can be loosely termed as 2020's very own apocalypse.

At the onset of the first wave, we were as uncertain about the longevity of the outbreak as the next person. However, over the course of living through it, conducting interviews and documenting stories surrounding it, we have come to understand the magnitude of its impact. With every narrative that we penned down, a news headline turned into a real person's life story, a grim statistic suddenly had a voice. The migrant worker exodus or the growing mortality rate in India, for example, were no longer just numbers, they were real stories of ongoing struggles. Each interview with a narrator took us deeper into a reality that we were never privy to.

Surprisingly, conversing about these ordeals proved more therapeutic than triggering—both for the narrators and us. Many of them noted that in the process of creating this book, they had the chance, for the first time, to share all the emotions and experiences they had been going through. Speaking to people felt cathartic, as it became an outlet for bottled-up emotions and overwhelming fear. It was comforting to vocalise the many apprehensions the narrators as well as we were going through. We had all experienced a sense of loss in different capacities, to different degrees—loss of opportunities, time, normalcy and, in some cases, lives. However, these interactions managed to rekindle hope. Knowing that it was a collective healing process gave us perspective and helped us cope with the gravity of the situation.

*

The trajectory of the pandemic has been far from linear. The period from December 2020 till March 2021 could have been classified as the resolution of the crisis. Health officials in certain states declared that Covid-19 was nearing the endemic phase. Delhi's health minister Satyendar Jain asserted that the situation was well within control in the national capital and that the infection rate was less than 1 per cent for two months consecutively. Life was slowly crawling towards normalcy with offices, restaurants, universities and schools finally opening up. This was, however, short-lived. Even as the vaccine trials proved successful, and India launched two vaccines—Covaxin and Covishield—the situation saw a drastic downturn.

By April 2021, another surge unfolded, and news surrounding the number of deaths caused by the virus continued to baffle us. Social media platforms were flooded with cries for help: someone searching for oxygen cylinders for their mother whose oxygen levels had dropped to 64, another desperately asking for a hospital bed for their ailing sister, yet another looking for plasma donations, etc. The second wave of Covid-19 in India was far worse than the first.

We live at one of the epicentres of the second wave: New Delhi. The country's capital suffered as hospitals survived on limited hours of oxygen supply. We heard news of close friends, family members and acquaintances experiencing the demise of their loved ones almost every day. Compared to 2020, we saw the fear of death and infection increase manifold. Each day, India saw a new record of Covid-19 cases and deaths. This soaring mortality rate meant that cremation grounds ran out of space. People had to resort to bidding farewell to their loved ones inside a parking lot or a makeshift pyre on a footpath. Students had to face cancelled examinations, virtual classes and a severe lack of jobs. Malls, cinema halls and other public spaces remained shut. It was 2020, all over again. *But much worse.*

This second wave of the virus reinforced the importance of writing this book. While the entire world was caught off guard during the first wave, India suffered the most during its second. Due to the stories and information that we had gathered for the book, we were able to see the progression of events and how the lives of the narrators, in particular, were further impacted.

*

Over the course of 2020–21, the pandemic has tested our resilience in the face of unimaginable, complex crises. When the virus first hit, the world was fired up by a greater cause: to fight this together. Every crisis has three phases: emergency, regression and, finally, recovery. And while recovery may seem like smooth sailing in comparison to manoeuvring through Covid-19, that too is often filled with something akin to withdrawal symptoms, loss and doubt. That's because during the emergency, the sense of purpose seems rather crystal clear: *Act now. Safeguard your business. Protect your loved ones. Take precautions. Stay hopeful.* As the recovery unfolds, more fundamental and nagging questions arise: *What comes after? What parts of your business and organisation will even be relevant in the future? What is the new big picture?* To address and answer these questions, we must focus on three areas: recognising that we are faced with a new, broader challenge, recalibrating our lives, and re-entering the world with contagious hope.

The pandemic has made us aware of our ability to cope with both professional and personal distresses. Millennials have been repeatedly called "the burnout generation", but the unpredictability of 2020 taught us that even the most well-laid-out plans can turn out to be fragile. In many ways, it was a cosmic correction disguised as a large-scale crisis. For many of us, it was a trigger to improvise, devise immediate solutions that work for us and hold ourselves accountable. It hit "pause" on our otherwise ambitious path to success and restored perspective. A tumultuous situation such as this one calls one to question: *what can we do to support our mental health, cultivate resilience and continue to grow in the face of so many new challenges*? Through these difficult times, the hope is that the stories of frontline workers, small business owners, those who lost their livelihoods and of ones belonging to the lower stratum of the society, will help people survive and thrive in the new normal.

Naturally, therefore, the accounts in this book also call attention to the unexpected high points brought on by the crisis. Circumstances engendered by the pandemic forced individuals to innovate and make decisions which they would not have under normal circumstances, which ended up having its own advantages. Chronically busy individuals started indulging in activities of personal growth, such as bonding with their family and taking up new hobbies. Working mothers, constantly juggling between work and raising their children, finally had the avenue (work-from-home) to strike some sort of balance, though the pandemic ushered in newer challenges. People across the world came together and formed small global virtual communities and built authentic relationships. Culturally, we have been catapulted to a future we could not have imagined, and strategically, our transformation has gained a momentum we may not have anticipated. Seasoned professionals from the entertainment industry recognise this period as a cultural renaissance that was a long time coming.

Slowly, almost unknowingly, everyday life will resemble what it used to, and a sense of routine will again set in. However, below the surface, there will still be turmoil. The pandemic came as a rupture but has seeped into our existence, irreversibly. Now, a constant hesitation accompanies actions and events that we once took for granted—hugging someone, entering a public place, making spontaneous travel plans, eating at a restaurant, etc. The impact of this pandemic cannot be quantified in a definitive manner due to the complexity it poses.

This collection of narratives is only a dip in the ocean of stories worth narrating. Some of the stories are happy, some heart-breaking, others inspirational, and then there are some that readers can instantly connect with. Equipped with curiosity and an intent to chronicle experiences, we hope, in future, to bring more unique experiences to add to this series.

We spoke to most of the contributors in the book in 2020. Hence, the facts and figures mentioned are indicative of the time period it was written in and in no way represents latest data. Over the past year, the twenty lives documented in this book have undergone emotional, mental and life-altering transformation. At the very beginning, both the duration and direness of this pandemic were unknown, and so was the length of this book. However, its purpose has remained intact throughout: to give an authentic voice to these stories of bravery, innovation and unflinching strength. As we live through this time, we strive to finish what we started: document modern history's most unimaginable time up to its very end, if there ever will be one.

1

Lights, Camera, Action: The Reel and the Real during Covid-19

Vidya Balan, Film Actor

Editors' Note

Once a generation, the world of movies, cinema and acting experiences a seismic shift. The year 2020 was when it happened again. Will movie-going survive the pandemic? The question sounds both trivial—there are surely graver matters to worry about—and unduly apocalyptic.

The streaming era has finally arrived, and everything is about to change. With more original movies bypassing big screens, the line between TV and film is blurring, prompting once-unthinkable questions. Studios, for instance, employ separate executive teams to oversee the development and production of movies and television series. Should that siloed approach end?

Whether cinemas survive or not, Disney and Netflix will find screens and viewers. Netflix, which is sprinkling some of its 2020 releases into theatres, has built a subscription empire on the belief that people would just as soon stay home and surrender to the algorithm. These two companies together control an ever-larger share of the global attention span, and their growing reach cannot help but raise troubling thoughts in a movie lover's mind.

What if the pandemic, rather than representing a temporary disruption in audience habits and industry revenues, turns out to be an extinction-level event for movie-going? What if, now that we've grown accustomed to watching movies in our living rooms or on our laptops, we lose our appetite for the experience of walking down carpeted hallways, trailing stray popcorn kernels and cradling giant cups of Coke Zero, to jostle for an aisle seat and hope all that soda doesn't mean we'll have to run to the bathroom during the big action sequence?

The onslaught is upending in almost every way how the Hindi film industry (and the film industry at large) does business. Actors, directors, producers and the 250-member crew required to put up a release-worthy movie, were suddenly declared jobless. How have they been spending their time? An entire profession that's used to travelling 300 days out of 365—how have they been tackling the mental turmoil of being stuck within the confines of their home? Do they like the downtime or are they waiting to claw their way back onto the glamorous sets of a Bollywood production?

Vidya Balan, one of Indian cinema's most seasoned actors, is known for pioneering a change in the way we perceive and watch movies. In this narrative, she shares her candid experience of living life through the global pandemic, her informed opinion on the future of films, and how she innovated to make the most of her time in hibernation.

*

The bulk of 2020 has felt like an interim between "lights, camera, action!" and "cut!" This pandemic has been a long waiting game. And waiting is a loaded act, one that demands metamorphosis. From fear and anxiety, the act of waiting transforms into an uneasy calm, which then develops into a sense of disappointment. Here, it stagnates and eventually transforms into frustration, but somehow reclaims the ability to revive hope. This crisis has made history and brought about a profound change for the Hindi film industry—we were one of the first to be affected and will probably be the last to recover.

The skills I've developed over the past fifteen years as an actor seem to have been repurposed for or projected onto my real life at this point. I have had to improvise every day for the past few months, just like I would have to on a movie set. I've transformed in the process, like I do for every character that I play. And exactly like a character in a film, I hope to eventually reach a happy ending.

Just when Covid-19 was at the cusp of being declared a global pandemic, I was already in isolation of sorts as I was shooting amidst the jungles of Madhya Pradesh for my film, *Sherni*. As one might imagine, the network coverage in the area was rather sporadic; stranded in the jungle, there was no convenient way of knowing or keeping up with what was going on in the world.

When we finally did get network, it turned out that what was going on outside the jungle was even more wild! We had to pause the shoot midway and head back home to Bombay, with no certainty of when we were to resume work. When I was travelling back to Bombay from Bhopal, I was taken aback seeing only a handful of people at the airport—fifty-six to be precise. I wasn't aware of all the facts concerning the pandemic and wondered if the world was overreacting. When we finally touched down in Bombay, it felt different, for the first time in forty-one years of my living here. Bombay didn't feel like

Bombay. A city that overcame bomb blasts, riots and floods seemed helpless in the face of this worldwide pandemic.

While I was still trying to make sense of the chaos around me, a nationwide lockdown was announced.

Believe it or not, my immediate fear was how we were to manage daily functions and logistics for the next twenty-one days. We hadn't stocked up to last that long! Our cook couldn't come to our house and the house-help who stayed with us wasn't a cook.

A nationwide lockdown meant that even the grocery stores wouldn't deliver anymore. The only choice was to step out myself for necessities—food and medicine. The last time I'd visited a grocery store was more than fifteen years ago. I'd never seen so many people in one shop; there was obvious anxiety everywhere. The feeling was all-encompassing. What lay ahead of us? It was my father's seventy-fifth birthday in a month. Would this twenty-one-day lockdown be extended? Would I be able to meet my father, who lives less than five minutes from me? Oh, and what about work? I had shoots lined up; I'd already said yes to one film apart from *Sherni* and was on the verge of committing to another. Every single plan, from the next day to the next couple of months, had to be redrawn.

A fond morning ritual of mine involves stepping into my balcony, looking at the beach, soaking it in, and being mesmerised at the sight every single time. The morning after the lockdown was announced, I stood in my balcony only to find that my morning sight wouldn't look the same for a while. Not a single soul was spotted at the once bustling beach filled with morning walkers, fishermen, lovers and families. Bombay, the city of dreams, the city that doesn't stop for anyone, the city that never sleeps, was eerily silent that day: it was deafening.

During pre-Covid times, my work was irregular; either I'd be shooting or promoting for days on end, or, once we'd wrap, I'd be free for a couple of weeks. In those weeks, I would spend a considerable amount of time at home. I'm a homebody, so staying indoors was never a cause for huge concern. In fact, that I often hibernate is a running joke among my friends and so practising isolation and social distancing was not an alien concept for me. However, the only difference in this case was that I was forced to stay indoors for days and eventually months at a stretch, whereas earlier I would choose to stay indoors.

After the initial weeks of lockdown, when we'd accepted the seemingly perpetual state of uncertainty, our altered everyday activities became the new routine. Siddharth (my husband) and I would divide the household chores alternating between sweeping and swabbing. It reminded us of how adaptable we can be. We always knew this, we still do, but it's times like these that reaffirm your faith in your ability to adjust, to change. For my husband and I, the process was new, but thankfully not impossible to carry out.

More importantly, the task of adapting goes beyond just the household and the individual. A huge part of who I am is the work I do but a paradigm shift had taken place in the world of cinema as well. There is no doubt that the crisis had come as a crippling blow to the film industry at large. Shoots were cancelled, sets dismantled, the backbone of the industry—the spot boys, stunt men, makeup artists, etc.—were out of work. After the theatres shut down, the challenge for our industry was to take the stories, the art of storytelling and the ensemble film viewing experience from the big screen to the small screen.

Releasing *Shakuntala Devi* on Prime Video allowed us to make the movie available to people across 200 countries at once. It's common knowledge that releasing a film is a long, tedious process involving years of hard work. Often, films get shelved, or a complete product is jaded by the time it sees the light of theatres. Therefore, the very fact that films now have another avenue is a blessing. Streaming platforms are not just a cost-effective alternative but are also deeply satisfying for everyone involved in the production of a piece—actors, producers and crew members. After all, your content is as good as what your audience makes of it. The more eyeballs we attract, the more the possibility of a balanced review. The surging reliance on direct-to-home distribution is encouraging producers to experiment with genres and storylines that don't fit the traditional formula for Indian fare. Rather than witnessing the end of the big box office numbers, we're seeing a broadening of the horizon. In this new, more diverse landscape, there will be greater space for experimentation and novelty (and failure), and filmmakers are already trying their hand at new formats. There is so much you can't show on the big screen, for reasons as straightforward as "it's not theatrical enough".

Every viewer is bound to have a different relationship with the content they watch. Services like OTT platforms give them the chance to choose when, where and with whom they watch the movie, if with anyone at all. Bollywood film studios are known to produce the largest number of movies in the world annually. Even though pandemic restrictions have put our business model to the test, the revolution of streaming platforms has led to the democratisation of the movie viewing experience.

Another crucial aspect of film budgets is promotions. Yes, contrary to popular opinion, I'm guilty of enjoying promotions. This time around, however, surprisingly, I enjoyed them more from behind the screen. Earlier, journalists would come to Mehboob Studios or one of our regular promotional haunts, with a predictable set of questions in hand. You simply knew what was going to happen.

Interestingly, I happened to be among the first to promote my work online, and when I was promoting *Shakuntala Devi*, I noticed a certain freshness in the process. Unlike before, where I was aware of the kind of questions I'd be asked, there were varied questions for which I wasn't even prepared. That truly made the nature of interviews more enjoyable.

Having said that, it was also undeniably exhausting. Earlier, as you needed to travel to various venues for promotions, there was time to breathe. But in this case, there was one designated spot at home where all the interviews took place, so they were scheduled immediately one after the other.

The tedium of being hooked to a screen finally saw an end when things started opening up. With each phase of the easing of restrictions, we crawled towards normalcy. I was also called to resume shooting. As one might imagine, a film set looked nothing like it did before. Everyone, myself included, was more cautious than ever, a tinge of paranoia accompanying the caution. No one wants to take the virus lightly because the data surrounding the number of Covid cases and deaths escalated by the day. We have a Covid management team on set, which ensures that all the necessary protocols are being followed. There are daily temperature checks and inspections regarding masks being worn properly and to see that no one is breaking the bio-bubble. In addition to the visible changes, there's a sense of caution among the crew.

A key parting perspective from the Covid-19 pandemic and consequent lockdown is the strong case it has made for a simple lifestyle amid an atmosphere of alarming recession, foreclosures, joblessness and underemployment. The value of a decluttered life is gradually making sense to many of us. During lockdown or home quarantine, the most prodigal spendthrifts among us have begun to learn or at least show interest in the benefits of minimalism. We had become a world of excesses. But in order to keep safe and secure in an unpredictable atmosphere of disease, death, deprivation and utter helplessness, we have been able to easily forgo most pleasures that once felt like necessities. We have, maybe momentarily, bid farewell to gyms and workout centres and are making do with freehand exercises or yoga asanas, sitting on the modest mat at home. Instead of sumptuous lunches or dinners at expensive hotels or restaurants, we are now satisfied with recipes sans frills at home that are made hygienically.

Another by-product of this crisis was the time it gave me to pause and introspect. It made me realise that you didn't need all that much in life. Sometimes this lockdown reminded me of how, centuries ago, life was lived in a cave with a partner and not much more. Maybe our natural instincts are now dominating our consumerist selves. For that, and for so much more, I'm really thankful. In fact, in the past six months, I experienced gratitude in a way like never before—for finally learning how to cook, for getting to share the pleasures (and pains) of doing household chores with Siddharth, for this uncalled-for yet necessary evolution that this crisis has served the Indian film industry, and for learning how to come to terms with spontaneity. I am a stringent planner, from calendaring my travel to setting daily schedules. I was not cut out to deal with the precariousness this pandemic forced upon us. But somehow, in dealing with this nationwide lockdown and pandemic, I've found a way to take every day as it is and trust in my ability to be self-reliant.

Being an actor may seem all pomp and splendour from afar, but when it comes down to the nitty-gritty, a crisis like this acts as a leveller. This crisis has affected all of us, in ways that may or may not be comparable. That we had to fight the battle in unity, gives me solace.

2

Digging Deeper Wounds

Mohammad Shameem, Gravedigger

Editors' Note

With the advent of the novel coronavirus, death statistics and mortality rates have become a part of our dailiness, with lives lost becoming just a statistic, a peak on a graph. The process of handling dead bodies in Indian culture, across religions, is long drawn out. Very rarely do we pause and think about the people who carry out the tasks of burial, who collect the ashes after cremation and procure bodies from hospitals and morgues. It thus becomes imperative to tell the stories of those involved in handling the ground realities of burial and cremation, and whose stories barely get told due to their position in society.

Belonging to a family of Indian cemetery workers, Mohammad Shameem had little choice when it came to his profession. A day at his job during the pandemic included the following: he gets a call from a hospital informing him of Covid-19 infected corpses, he procures the bodies and performs the last rites. He gets paid Rs 100 per body. His job wasn't easy even in the pre-pandemic world. However, it's even worse now as Shameem and the people from his profession are wrongfully accused of carrying the infection. His story provides an unfiltered view into the state of the labour class in a global pandemic.

It is an account of how the looming threat of infection, uncertainty of income, the overall gloom and overwhelmingness associated with performing the last rites of unknown people make his "new normal" distinct from ours.

*

"*Mera naam Mohammad Shameem hai, aur main Dilli ke Jadid Qabristan Ahle Islam mein kaam karta hun.*" (My name is Mohammad Shameem and I work in Delhi's Jadid Qabristan Ahle Islam).

I come from a family of gravediggers. My grandfather, Shahbuddin, my father and I have spent our lives working on the same burial ground. My grandfather would take my father to the cemetery every day. My father would go there and spend his entire day observing my grandfather carry out the process of burying dead bodies. This is not a task that one can learn overnight where one person dictates and the other is expected to follow. Therefore, my grandfather made sure that my father accompanied him every day for nearly a year-and-a-half until he learned and was capable of carrying the burial out himself.

I was around sixteen years old when I was told that I would have to do this job as well. Honestly, I was never inclined towards it. I did not want to be a gravedigger. Whenever I'd tell my friends that I lived in a cemetery or told my teacher that my father worked at a burial ground, they would instantly frown or look at me differently. Their behaviour made me think of this profession as a curse.

Noticing my vehement refusal to do this job, my father sat me down one day and said, "*Beta, jo hum karte hain, yeh toh punya ka kaam hai.*" He said that our work was in accordance with God's will; it accomplished good and is necessary, even if it comes without the deserved recognition. He motivated me to reconsider my decision by offering a perspective I'd not been privy to. His words were powerful and came from a place of sincerity. Following our conversation, I decided to become a gravedigger.

In Islam, the body is first fully washed at home and enshrouded in a white cloth. Then namaz is read and finally, the body is put to rest inside the grave. I remember when I first buried a dead body. Nearly 400 people were present at the site and I was petrified. Everyone was in mourning and I did not want to mishandle the body or falter in the process to make things worse. However, fortunately, I followed all the necessary steps involved and there were no issues. Since that day, this has been my job and I know everything there is to know and do. Or so I thought, until the pandemic hit.

I always had my grandfather or father's experience to rely on, if I had any questions regarding my profession. But none of them had witnessed what I'm witnessing right now—a global pandemic. My workplace and my job that was so familiar to me, started becoming alien. How do you bury a body without touching or seeing it? The 44-acre graveyard that was started in 1924 now looked and felt like a war zone.

Other gravediggers who had also been working in this graveyard refused to do their job for the first time in a hundred years. They refused to dig graves for Covid-19 victims and only stuck to burying regular bodies. So, it was only Wasim (the imam) and I, standing on the 2-acre land, burying Covid-19 bodies on our own.

With over one lakh fifty thousand reported deaths caused by Covid-19, the fatigue of being a gravedigger started to become more apparent. Wasim was the only imam present and hence the only one to offer prayers for the departed soul. As a result, the process of burial sometimes extended well beyond the usual timeframe. But his mantra that "fear cannot be greater than humanity" kept him going even under such testing circumstances.

Sometimes it feels like democracy is a privilege only the rich can afford. People like me, and jobs like mine are taken for granted. Our work is often termed "disposable" or "replaceable" with very little consideration given to those who are actually doing it. Truth be told, if we don't do this, no one else would.

Each time a Covid-19 infected body was brought to the graveyard, the same argument ensued over the cursed question: who will unload it from the vehicle and take it to the burial spot? The deceased's immediate family members, relatives and hospital staff—not one of them wanted to touch the body. Some families left even before the body had been unloaded. It infuriated me. If people are afraid to touch their own deceased relatives, why should I? Some people did not even show up for the burial and instead asked me to coordinate with the hospital and take care of all the formalities. They only requested that we show them the burial via video call. In exchange, they transferred some money via Paytm. It felt extremely weird to suddenly see the number of people present at a qabristan go down from nearly 400 to zero.

While this was the situation for Shameem in the national capital, one could only imagine the state in smaller villages or towns. In Delhi, where there was still manpower and tractors present to make the burial process easier, the plight of a gravedigger in a small village of

Uttar Pradesh was similar in essence but also different. Iqbal works at the Nigran Shah graveyard in Uttar Pradesh. He digs graves for both Covid and non-Covid patients. He says, "Digging a grave is not easy. It requires energy. Usually, it takes three hours for two men to dig one grave, but I do it alone. The grave has to be of appropriate dimensions. I double-check the dimensions before the body arrives because this is serious work." Describing the change he experienced due the pandemic, Iqbal says, "Many people stop loving their family members once they discover that they are coronavirus patients. The stigma is more harmful to society than the virus. Coronavirus has revealed an insensitive side of humans. I have now lost the count of graves that I have dug till date."

You might wonder if I have the right to be upset. After all, it *is* my job. But Covid-19 changed the demands my job made of me. I felt like a participant in a psychological experiment—only, my consent wasn't mine. It was being forced out of me because of the simple reason that no one else was willing to do the job. Except for a few media channels, there was no platform that cared about the mental turmoil of being a gravedigger in a worldwide pandemic. There was nothing in the rulebook mandating I had to touch a body affected by Covid-19. In fact, we were repeatedly encouraged to maintain our distance and direct people from afar. The World Health Organization (WHO) guidelines clearly stated that healthcare workers or mortuary staff preparing the body (for e.g., washing the body, tidying hair, trimming nails, or shaving) should wear appropriate personal protective equipment (PPE) according to standard guidelines. We were barely provided with any of that. However, when the situation was as deadly as it was and one was gambling with something as big as life itself, I thought about safety too. Especially when acclaimed news channels reported that autopsies of Covid-19 bodies have revealed that the virus can remain active for several hours after an infected person has died.

When we received the first Covid-19 infected dead body, our families clearly asked us to not pursue this work. My family of five and I were petrified. My four children and my wife desperately tried convincing me not to work. "We will stop meeting you, cooking for you, washing your clothes for you and will not let you inside the house," they said. The risk was such that going to work could not be justified. Hence, I adamantly refused the officials from our village committee on continuing to work. But it didn't end there.

I, along with my gravedigger partner, was taken to meet a doctor from Ram Manohar Lohia Hospital. They detailed the situation for us. "Shameem, this virus exists inside the body, not outside or on the surface. If you take the necessary precautions (sanitise yourself after performing the burial), there is no way for you to be infected. When you receive the body, it is dead. When we receive it, it's still breathing. So is the virus inside it. When the person speaks or coughs or sneezes, we stand at a risk of catching the infection. However, you will receive the sanitised body packed in a sealed bag." Based on his professional opinion, he told us that we could (and should) do the work. He did advise us to maintain our distance from the body and take necessary precautions. We were told they would assign a health worker to touch the bodies—we were to only guide them from afar.

None of the other qabristans in Delhi were willing to take this job up. Everyone had made up their minds. "They have lost all humanity," they explained to us. We were Muslims and the body that had arrived was of a Muslim too. The question ensued, "If you don't do it, who will?" They promised to provide us with anything we may require along the way. After he finished explaining this to us, the area's senior officials came to visit us as well. By the time they finished speaking with us, it stopped being a question of "if I wanted to do it" but rather, "when will I be ready to begin?" After that, the doctor patiently explained the science of transmission and was physically present for the burial of the first Covid-19 dead body.

When I took up the job, my wife and my parents weren't supportive—and rightly so. They weren't even speaking with me, except for taunting me: "Will you win an award for doing this?" or "Will they pay you huge amounts of money?" My wife didn't send any food for me during the first three days. I was relying on the packaged food sent to the entire area by Delhi Police for free.

Every morning, starting at 9, my phone would ring off the hook with families, doctors and ambulance drivers informing me of their arrival at the qabristan. One ambulance contained a maximum of three to four bodies. First, two drivers wearing PPE kits would get off, inspect the area assigned for the burial and unload a white plastic bag with the body inside. A small piece of paper was attached to the bag that read the name of the deceased. Due to the contagiousness of the virus, one needed to avoid opening the sealed bag to identify the body. Therefore, family members had to make peace with not seeing their loved ones for one last time. Once everyone had arrived, the burial process would begin with the namaz, followed by the burial. During Covid times, the body needed to be tightened with ropes and then slowly lowered down into the 6-foot grave. Relatives who could not make it to the burial would see the process via video conferencing, which came closest to any kind of closure they would get.

For the next few months, I started going to my house only during the night, after I had showered and washed my clothes.

If I needed something during the day, my wife delivered it to me and would leave it on the doorstep. I had set up a small store next to my house where I kept my clothes and some bathing equipment. I spent most of my time there, pretty much by myself. The feeling was terrifying. I couldn't sleep during the nights. I would be awake in fear. It was surreal—after a long day of intensive physical work, how could I not fall asleep? I was scared. I cannot explain the feeling. I simply cannot. I had no human beings around me. At night or during the day, my interaction was limited to barely three people. It was a fatal loneliness. Waseem, the imam, and I heard that everyone was living in isolation, but in the comforts of their homes. Now, imagine having to robotically bury dead bodies for eight hours straight. No one could be where we were—physically or mentally.

I sent my children to stay with my parents, away from me. I would often watch the news on my phone and come across videos of service workers of other nations. The rising demand, panic buying, hoarding and misuse leading to shortages throughout the country. Without secure supply chains, the risk to workers was real. Initially, we received PPE kits, masks and sanitisers from the senior officials in the area. When the number of burials increased manifold and we were at a lack of resources, we started asking the relatives to provide the necessary safety equipment. We would arrange masks and sanitisers with the help of a few relatives, friends and, sometimes, the district head. We were on our own. And that was just the struggle for resources, but they may as well have said, "If you get the virus, it's on you." The way I looked at the situation was: it was impossible to stop the spread of Covid-19 without protecting the nation's service workers first.

Since the time of my grandfather's generation, we gravediggers have probably been burying a maximum of six bodies on any given day. By July 2020, my partner and I were burying fifteen to eighteen dead bodies every day. We would start at 9 a.m. sharp and bury bodies continuously up until 5 p.m., with a thirty-minute lunchbreak in the middle. The dreary sequence unfolded like this: we would get a call from the hospital at 9 a.m., informing us of the number of bodies they were sending. The relatives would either accompany them to the burial ground and hand it over to us, or sign a form declaring that they were shifting the responsibility of the body to the hospital staff. It was starting to take a toll on us, and soon, it became difficult for the hospital caretakers to manage. Things started slipping. About five to six times over the past few months, we have buried a Hindu on our ground, in violation of Hindu death rituals that require cremation. When the body arrives, all we know about the deceased person is their name. Sometimes, that isn't enough to identify whether the person was Hindu or Muslim.

One shocking incident that I vividly remember was when a Hindu body was brought to our qabristan and a Muslim body was taken to a Hindu crematorium. During the initial days, everything was chaotic and the fear of getting infected was greater than anything else. Every person who was part of the process—doctors, nurses, relatives, transportation people, and we gravediggers—just wanted to keep ourselves safe. One day, a little girl came to attend her mother's burial. Usually, no one was allowed to open the sealed bag that contained the body. But the girl insisted and begged to see her mother one last time. How could I have said no? A child was requesting to see her dead mother. Giving into her innocent and sincere request, I decided to open the bag from afar. To everyone's utter shock, it was not her mother. We immediately alerted authorities and found out that there was a mistake. Two bodies had left the same hospital but the Hindu one landed up in the qabristan while the Muslim one had reached the *shamshaan ghat*. Upon calling the *shamshaan ghat*, we found that the girl's mother had already been burnt. I still cannot forget the girl's face. She could not see her mother for the last time or get any kind of closure. She cried uncontrollably, and the sight was gut-wrenching. I still remember her face and that she was from Bareilly, a district in Uttar Pradesh.

Another such incident was when I received a call from a doctor at AIIMS who asked me for help in burying an unidentified dead body. The cause of this man's death was Covid-19. The deceased was a Muslim and deserved a traditional, dignified burial. If we refused to do it, chances were he would have been cremated. On 8 October, a police official brought the body to the graveyard. I buried the body and even had to pay Rs 2,000 for the arrangements as the family was not around. Ever since the outbreak of Covid-19, I have buried six to seven such dead bodies; their families or origins were never traced.

The very land we work on speaks volumes about the amount of deaths we have seen. The cemetery used to span about 2 acres, 50 per cent of which was used up by June of 2020. This was just four months after the lockdown was announced. Initially, only about one-fourth of the burial ground was allotted to Covid-19 burials. By September 2020, the government had to increase the total burial ground by 3 acres, and the area allotted to Covid-19 burials increased four times. It became evident to us that there was a considerable gap between the number of deaths shown on the news and the actual number of deaths. Only the people who had tested positive for Covid-19 were counted in the total national tally flashed on the news every day. The ones that were merely suspected were not counted but buried under the Covid-19 allotted spaces in the cemetery. The cemetery was at full capacity for the first time. With the way things were moving, I thought we would need to clear even the last remaining patch of land for graves in the coming months.

But it wasn't just the rise in the number of deaths that complicated our jobs. Following the strict and necessary protocols itself became a challenge. We now wear PPE kits while burying bodies. A typical PPE kit consists of a full bodysuit, one pair of disposable fog-safe eye goggles, a three-ply disposable face mask, surgical gloves, cap, shoe covers and disposable bags. It is also worn by healthcare workers, people taking care of infected people or by others who need to protect themselves from infection. It's made using SMS 90 GSM fabric that is impermeable. Most other workers who wear the kit were stationed in air-conditioned hospitals, offices or houses. We, on the other hand, were in the middle of a jungle, where the temperature peaked at 102°F during the day. It was impossible to wear the kit for longer than two burials without having to wipe the sweat off our body. The municipal officials provided thirty PPE kits for the burials but just within a week, we ran out of them.

WHO stated that the graves meant for coronavirus victims would have to be at least 6 feet deep. I had to resort to my wooden stick to measure this depth. Cemeteries in industrialised countries, however, provide backhoe loaders or other heavy equipment that makes the process a lot more accurate and much less cumbersome.

While the usual cost of digging a grave is a few hundred rupees, Christian families had been shelling out high sums for coffins. A sixty-eight-year-old man, Namdeo Sangle, was laid to rest a day after he died at Nair Hospital. His family spent Rs 20,800 to hire three gravediggers from Borivali to bury him at Sewri Christian Cemetery. These men were also ambulance drivers. PPE kits had to be arranged for them. The diggers initially asked for Rs 22,000, but the family pleaded and settled it for Rs 20,800. The diggers travelled 30 km from Borivali to Sewri, and Namdeo was finally buried. Another family, in Bandra (Mumbai), faced a similar harrowing time when the administration at St Andrews Church initially refused to bury their family member. Upon informing them that BMC (Bombay Municipal Corporation) rules allow burial of a Covid-19 body, they agreed. They had to pay Rs 15,000 to find gravediggers who were willing to touch the dead body. A coffin usually costs Rs 4,000 to 6,000. Community members said that burials had turned into a money-minting business; coffin providers began offering a package fee for PPE, gravediggers and coffins. People were helpless and had no other option but to pay these exorbitant charges.

A growing number of Christian families were finding it excruciating to undertake traditional funeral rites of Covid-19 victims, majorly due to the absence of gravediggers in Mumbai. Not only did they have to call for gravediggers from outside (at a very high cost), but they also had to fight with the management of the cemeteries to provide some space. Even if they did provide space, it was the family's job to arrange a coffin and gravediggers.

Today is 22 September 2020. It has been seven months since I hugged my wife and showed my children any physical affection; for seven months uninfected people have been feeling petrified in my presence. Whenever Wasim and I would take a break and go for tea, the shopkeeper would greet us with death stares. Looking at our gloves and masks, he'd hesitate to even come near us. One would understand if the hesitation came from a sense of precaution, but this one reeked of discrimination. It's almost as if, actually, it's *exactly* as if I had contaminated the place.

Here's what being a gravedigger felt like during the Covid-19 pandemic. The incessant pressure, unprecedented levels of stress and uncertainty, and the constant exposure to death are all-exhausting. It has put my mental health in jeopardy. At some point, I felt like I had insomnia. Other days, I was too exhausted to cook my own meals. Soon, I lost my appetite. We hear that people get sick if they are overexposed to this virus. No one talks about how psychologically ill you become if you're overexposed to these stressors.

I have buried 600 Covid-19 infected (or suspected to be infected) dead bodies by far. I have not been infected with the virus yet. I hope to God that we all emerge from this soon, and I can sleep in the same house as my wife and kids, and go to work without the fear of dying. It is now going to be almost a year since India's first nationwide lockdown, and it makes me proud that things are considerably better than they were when this started. The country has made phenomenal progress in terms of mitigating the number of deaths caused by Covid-19. Now, we receive one body every three days, or five days, or a week. We have also filed the paperwork (Aadhar card) required to get vaccinated. Once our turn comes, we will get vaccinated.

The Quran states that all of us are made out of dust and will eventually go back to dust. But working with the dead has only taught us that no matter who you are, you will leave the world empty-handed. This belief led us to take the challenge head-on and do what had to be done.

3

A Lockdown "Workaholic"

Shashi Tharoor, Member of Parliament, Lok Sabha

Editors' Note

With great power comes great responsibility. The onus of decision-making and devising effective measures to manage a crisis falls on the shoulders of politicians—the policymakers and the executors. Citizens pin their hopes, fears and trust on those who have been chosen by them and for them. Countries that were seeing soaring Covid-19 cases such as Spain, Italy, France, etc., immediately called for a nationwide lockdown. While many praised India's early announcement for a lockdown, various states within India fared differently in terms of their approach and strategy to tackle the coronavirus.

Kerala was one of the first states in the country to beef up internal borders, establishing measures such as taking the temperature of passengers in cars. Using GPS technology, CCTV footage and mobile phone records to trace the movements of the first family to be infected in the state, they were quick to take effective action.

The state's strategy, also referred to as "The Kerala Model", was one of the first to succeed in the country and was replicated in other states. Shashi Tharoor, a member of parliament and the author, most recently, of The Hindu Way: An Introduction to Hinduism, *spearheaded the effort to provide relief to those affected by Covid-19, in Kerala and across India.*

In the following narrative, Tharoor shares insights into the political workings of India's response to the global pandemic. He further introspects the impact that the lockdown has had on his work. From detailing his most memorable incidents of the lockdown, to opening up about his lockdown activities (playing badminton, in particular), the world-renowned author takes us on an emotional journey, sprinkled with bouts of information and candour—all with the Tharoor touch.

*

Chronically busy people are busy all the time, any time: that's why their busy-ness is a chronic condition, like rheumatism or indigestion. I've been diagnosed with this malady in my childhood, before the word "workaholic" was invented. I've never known a moment of idleness since I was a toddler; I've always been mystified by people saying they were "bored", since I had no personal experience of boredom. All my life, there has always been more that I wanted to do than I had time for, which is why there was some curiosity among family, staff and friends when the lockdown was announced. Opinion seemed broadly divided into two camps: those who said, "Shashi can finally find time for all the things he's kept pending", and a sceptical minority who murmured, "Maybe Shashi will finally learn to relax."

The subtext in both cases, however, was, "Bet Shashi will still manage to be busy…"

For someone who had been insanely busy—travelling to thirteen different cities between 3 January and the opening of

Parliament on 1 February, hurtling to the constituency every weekend after a full schedule in the national capital, making speeches, attending events and meeting importunate visitors during the hours I was out of the House during the session—lockdown meant a life without any of the three main things that had kept me busy thus far: meetings, events and travel. Surely, this would help me ease up on my busy-ness?

Within a day or two, it became apparent that this would not be the case. Immediately, a huge amount of covid-related work, especially pertaining to the constituency, arose. On the evening Parliament adjourned, I had requested the prime minister, in the presence of the Lok Sabha Speaker, to amend the rules to permit MP funds under the Member of Parliament Local Area Development Scheme (MPLADS) to be used for essential supplies to combat Covid-19. On the first day of lockdown, the Speaker called me while I was at lunch: my proposal had been accepted; a revised order would be issued. My team in Thiruvananthapuram and I immediately swung into action, eliciting, from the local chapter of the Indian Medical Association (IMA) and the district collector, information about the things that were in short supply and urgently needed. We then immediately issued purchase orders under MPLADS for these essential items—9,000 kits of PPE for healthcare workers, 3,000 rapid-testing RT-PCR kits from the only lab in India approved to make them (Mylab in Pune), 250 non-contact thermometers from Hong Kong. The Sree Chitra Tirunal Institute for Medical Sciences in Thiruvananthapuram was doing cutting-edge research into a new RT-LAMP testing system for Covid-19: I allotted them a crore of rupees to complete their development, testing and manufacture of these kits for constituency use. And finally, with every rupee left in my available funds, I purchased a thermal face-detecting scanner to be installed at the airport to quickly detect passengers arriving with fever. No sooner had that order been placed than the prime minister announced the suspension of all MPLADS funds for two years: instead of funds being allotted by the local MP on the basis of awareness of local conditions and needs, they would now be sequestered by the central government, a reinforcement of a pattern of centralisation that has become all too apparent under the Modi regime.

But there were plenty of other things to do for the MP from Thiruvananthapuram. Keralites stranded abroad and wanting to come home reached out to me in large numbers from twenty-two countries (at last count)—ranging from students in places as far apart as Ukraine and the Philippines, to fishermen stranded in Iran by the lockdown, to businessmen unable to return home from what was intended to be a short business trip to a foreign country. Responding to their requests and bringing them to the attention of the authorities dealing with such problems took time. Then there were the people from elsewhere stuck in Kerala, whose MPs reached out to me for assistance. Social media brought me queries from political leaders in Bihar, Bengal, Maharashtra, and even Nagaland for such temporary migrants, for all of whom my constituency team arranged help. Another request was to record messages in Hindi and Bengali for migrant workers in Kerala at the request of the Malayala Manorama media house, which turned out to be effective in reassuring them and discouraging their attempted return to their home states. The Bengali message in particular—carefully crafted by this former Kolkatan in some trepidation—went viral, since many people could not imagine a Kerala MP speaking Bengali!

And then came what family referred to as the "typically Shashi Tharoor" invitations, for video conferences and interviews on the virus, to preparing and delivering a series of five hour-long lectures for the online education portal Unacademy, and speaking in a large number of "webinars" addressing varied audiences on various subjects, from my books to my life to the possible future shape of the post-covid world. These have averaged two a day throughout the lockdown, sometimes more, occasionally less. As occasions that would normally have been commemorated by events assumed "virtual" form, various requests for video messages poured in, and I devote some time a day to recording goodwill greetings to inaugurate seminars, celebrate landmark anniversaries or hail occasions like Earth Day and International Nurses Day. Planned efforts to revive the All-India Professionals' Congress, which I lead, have been forced to assume a "virtual" form, but have been taking shape through Zoom conferences and phone calls. And covid continued to intrude on the rest of my time, since I inevitably spent hours studying the policy questions, reading about the experiences of other countries, or speaking to, and issuing letters to, ministers on those issues that affected my constituents.

But there was some relief from covid work as well. As it happened, my mother and a sister (who lives in London) are locked down with me too. My mother, who maintains an independent life in Kochi, though she has thankfully been spending more and more time with me in Delhi, was scheduled to go back on 15 March 2020, and my sister, who was on a work trip in India, was supposed to accompany her before returning to London a week later. An hour before they left for the airport, I stopped them from going. I had been admonished, publicly and privately, by my sons and concerned relatives for continuing my regular work and not taking the dangers of the pandemic seriously enough.

Suddenly, at the eleventh hour, I just didn't feel comfortable letting my mother out of my sight with a possible coronavirus crisis about. I rarely make impulsive or instinctive decisions, but this was one I would be grateful for when the lockdown came.

The bonus of their presence was the kind of family time I had not enjoyed in most of my adult life. I feel guilty mentioning such private pleasures when so many of our countrymen and women have suffered terribly in the lockdown, and I realise this bonus came because of the privilege of being an MP with staff in residence, but that is my reality. We begin the day with morning tea together (and after the first phase of the lockdown, newspapers as well); make it a point to commune at mealtimes; and every evening, from about 7.30 or 8 (depending on that day's videoconferencing commitment) I spend a couple of hours with them, playing rummy or Scrabble, or watching something on television, often—thanks to my sister's subscription to the National Theatre in London—outstanding video recordings of astonishing stage productions there (These included a breathtaking *Frankenstein* with Benedict Cumberbatch, and *Antony and Cleopatra*, with Ralph Fiennes playing a part I had assayed in my last year of college at St Stephen's, opposite Mira Nair as the Egyptian queen. An inspiring and somewhat humbling viewing experience!)

My sister also made sure that I overcame my usual physical indolence and put in the time needed for regular exercise. Our healthcare workers are enduring enough strains: the least the rest of us can do is to keep ourselves fit and healthy, so as not to add to their burdens. She herself works out for an hour-and-a-half each day and goaded, nagged and exhorted me to do the same. The results have been, if not visibly spectacular, quietly impressive, and it is a habit I hope I can retain in a post-covid life. I was also able to engage my domestic staff and their children in impromptu games of cricket and badminton on the lawn, a great bonus of sarkari-bungalow life that I would never have been able to make time for pre-lockdown.

That I could be outdoors at all was thanks to another facet of the lockdown: the bright blue skies and cleaner air we have all been allowed to enjoy. The national capital region, the poster child of India's chronic, yearlong and nationwide air pollution problem—which on average sees most of the days in a year in the 'poor' to 'severe' category on the national Air Quality Index—has witnessed little short of an unimaginable miracle. With the lockdown in effect, and construction, industrial and vehicular activity (which cumulatively contribute 75 per cent of Delhi's PM 2.5 levels) down to a crawl, the capital has been experiencing record levels of clean air. Barring a single day on the fifth of April when a few overzealous supporters of the prime minister chose to take the latter's call to light lamps in support of our critical service providers to the next level by bursting firecrackers (and the lingering effects of their effusions the next morning), AQI levels in the city had dropped to scarcely believable levels. It has been truly refreshing to see AQI below 30 most days, on one occasion dropping into single digits—7! In Delhi! After an unexpected summer shower.

The net result of all my lockdown activity (as I write this on Day 42 of the third phase of the national lockdown) is that it's not a case of "all work and no play", even if this sounds like the schedule of a "dull boy": I am working sixteen-to-seventeen-hour days, of which eight to ten hours go on covid-related and constituency-connected work (including social media posts!), three to four hours on video conferences/webinars, Zoom meetings and interviews, one-and-a-half on exercise, two to three hours on mealtimes and family, and the remainder, whenever possible, on writing. I took the opportunity to conclude work that had already been well advanced on *Tharoorosaurus*, a light, illustrated collection of largely underused words, from 'agathokakological' to 'zugzwang' (the title combines my name with 'tyrannosaurus', since so many are terrified of difficult words, and 'thesaurus', since people want to be able to look them up). And then I embarked on, and completed, a considerably more 'serious' book on nationalism.

There have been memorable incidents almost every day of the lockdown. My cook's wife gave birth to a healthy baby girl on 14 April 2020, the day we Malayalis mark as the auspicious occasion of Vishu, and a rare Vishu when I was able to spend with family. Mother's Day was marked in my mother's company, which would not have happened but for the lockdown. (However, my treat for her—delivered food from a high-class eatery—misfired when the scheduled 1 p.m. delivery actually arrived at 3 p.m., delayed by various obstructions en route.) More unhappily, early in the lockdown, I discovered a major termite infestation had returned to the bookshelves in my study and devoured most of my precious collection of volumes on Nehru, Gandhi and Patel, which shared a shelf, many of which are out of print and irreplaceable.

There were heart-warming moments too: the seriously ill woman I was able to get a private room for at a hospital, the salaried patient whose savings had all been eaten up by treatment but for whose family I was able to negotiate a modest discount, the stranded travellers I was able to win priority for from a beleaguered government. (Fulsome tribute is due to Foreign Minister Jaishankar and Civil Aviation Minister Hardeep Puri, both old friends from their diplomatic days, who have been models of responsiveness and helpfulness amid their impossible schedules.)

The one lockdown experience that particularly comes to mind when I look back on these six weeks is when a distraught mother appealed to me about her infant daughter suffering a rare disease, for which the only cure lay in an experimental treatment in the Netherlands. The child's blood sample was to be rushed to the Netherlands for genetic analysis and then the treatment had to start before she turned two in June. With the lockdown and the flight cancellations, this had become impossible, and the mother was distraught. I spoke personally to the foreign minister and the civil aviation minister. They went out of their way not only to arrange to transport the sample, packed in dry ice, to Mumbai and then to the Netherlands, but to have it delivered by our embassy directly to the lab there in record time.

This humanity is ultimately what this entire national lockdown is all about—saving lives, helping each other, keeping our heads above the engulfing tide.

4

When Duty Calls, You Answer

Cabin Crew Member, Air India, Vande Bharat Mission

Editors' Note

As the battle against the SARS-CoV-2 virus took its toll on the global economy, no industry was hit harder than aviation. As reported by Harvard Business Review, BBC News and many other media platforms, this was the biggest crisis the aviation industry had ever faced. Airlines found ancillary revenue by unbundling services and selling à la carte things like checked baggage fees, seat selection, and so on. The source of revenue from these was close to zero because the number of passengers travelling had plummeted. Airlines were also looking to find any use for their aircraft in the absence of passengers, whether it be cargo or moving medical supplies and personnel to different markets. Many experts have also alluded to innovation in the future, to ensure peace of mind for passengers.

In the long run, the aviation industry expects to see the introduction of technologies to increase hygiene. Touchless seats that connect to Bluetooth on your phone to lower your back seat or fold out your tray; touchless lavatories; more regimented boarding procedures so there is no contact in the aisles. At airports, we expect to see facial recognition technology and tracking through customs and boarding, so customers and staff aren't touching the same boarding pass. While these changes will be positive from a passenger's point of view, they come at the risk of taking away from the thrill of flying. We've already seen airlines pulling the in-flight entertainment system out of the backs of the seats.

Private Indian airlines were hit hard. Vistara's (a leading Indian private airline—a joint venture between Tata Sons and Singapore Airlines) CEO took a 20 per cent salary cut up until December 2020, as we approached a vaccine. The rest of Vistara's senior staff, including members of the management, took a 15 per cent pay cut as well. Another leading airline, IndiGo, decided to lay off 10 per cent of its workforce, as reported by its CEO. SpiceJet reported a Rs 600 crore loss in its June quarter.

In order to tackle the spread of the coronavirus, sudden travel restrictions were put in place around the world. As a result, families, students, working professionals, tourists, etc., were rendered helpless, far from their home countries. On 7 May 2020, more than a month into the first nationwide lockdown in India, the government announced the Vande Bharat Mission. Numerous international and domestic evacuations were carried out in seven phases by both the central and state governments to bring back stranded Indians in different parts of the world during the global pandemic. More than 9,000 flights carrying over 11,98,660 passengers flew across twenty-two countries with only one aim—to repatriate Indians.

This is the story of a cabin crew member who flew across nations without hesitation to fulfil her duty when the nation demanded it. This came at the cost of putting herself and her family at risk. But when asked if she would do it all over again, her smile is answer enough. Many pilots, airhostesses, stewards, ground staff and the entire civil aviation administration within Air India and Indigo had to come together in making the Vande Bharat Mission a success. Employees worked tirelessly despite facing huge salary cuts. However, the larger challenge posed by the pandemic outweighed all other factors and encouraged them to play their role diligently.

This story relates the experience of working on the frontline. In addition, it makes a larger commentary on the manner in which air travel has transformed for the foreseeable future.

*

My husband is an army officer, and I am a cabin crew member for the flagship carrier airline of India—Air India. Given the context of our professions, stability or a sense of permanence is a fairly foreign concept for us. Our children have grown up knowing that very well. Be it parent–teacher meetings or attending annual functions, we divide parental duties to ensure that at least one parent can be present at these events. I was just nineteen when I applied for an interview to become an airhostess and since then, there has been no looking back. After earning my Bachelor of Arts degree with economics, public administration and political science, my first job was with Air India. And thirty-one years later, I'm still here. I am now at a managerial position with the airline.

Part of the thrill in what I do lies in travelling, visiting new places and meeting new people. My schedule would always be jam-packed, where six out of the seven days in a week, I'd be flying. It was hectic, with barely any leaves or time to take out for oneself. With my erratic schedule and that of my husband's in the army, my kids naturally grew independent fairly early on in life. They knew that for their dad, the nation comes before anyone or anything else. They also understand that for their mom, a huge part of her belongs to her service. While both jobs come with their own set of risks and uncertainties, they also bring a lot of pride.

The first time in the history of my service where I got a decently long enough break was during the lockdown. When the news was first announced, I was on a flight. I was terrified at what was happening to our country—the country that I've been serving for the past thirty-one years. I was petrified but hopeful, because I had faith in our ability to fight this as a nation. However, my tired eyes and exhausted brain couldn't help but think, "Oh, I'm finally going to get some time off!" Imagining a month-long staycation with my normal schedule would have been too ambitious, but in this case, I was told to stay home. I felt a temporary relief and calm, but I continued working, managing portfolios and carrying out remote work. I wanted to help the country fight this in whatever capacity I could.

The pandemic continued to sweep across the country. With no overnight flights, hectic schedules, or odd sleeping hours, my life had fallen into a calm routine. The initial days felt rewarding. I could take time out for myself, do yoga and spend time with my family. But every night I went to bed, it felt like something was missing. It felt as though I wasn't entirely complete despite having craved this break for three decades of my service. What was it that I was missing?

I got that answer a month into the lockdown. One day, as I sat at the dining table with my husband and kids, my phone rang. "We need you to report for the Vande Bharat rescue flight scheduled for London."

I took a second and looked at my husband. He raised his eyebrow in a bid to ask who was on the call.

"I'll be there," I said into the phone and the call ended.

In that brief pause, I thought of the peace I'd experienced staying at home all these days, and how many in London would be yearning for the same—to return to their loved ones, to return home. That thought changed my hesitant yes to a firm one. I had loved my time at home, but I was also excited to get back on the plane, all set to fly once again. And this time, it wasn't just for work. It was to bring hundreds of stranded Indians back home during a pandemic. If there was ever a time to put all my experience to good use, it was this.

The next morning, I woke up with electric energy. Although I was going on duty, it felt much more than just that; it felt like a mission. The morning of my first reporting for the Vande Bharat flight, I could feel a whole gamut of emotions running through my body. In this case, the risk was of getting infected, the uncertainty was about what's coming next, and the pride was about being part of doing something for the nation. I bid farewell to one family and made my way to the other—the one waiting for me on the runway.

I've been flying for years now, having clocked thousands of hours. Yet, never before in my life had I seen an emptier, more desolate flight. I walked into the aircraft, and all I could hear was the sound of the air conditioners. I saw empty seats that appeared almost ghostly. My job as a flight attendant primarily involves greeting people with a smile, serving them and being present at their beck and call. However, the biggest preventive measure for Covid-19 is reducing physical interaction. A middle ground of sorts was reached: my smile was now hidden behind the polyester of my PPE; passenger-crew interaction became bare minimum, to be avoided unless it was an emergency.

The flight from Delhi to London was nine hours long. But each second seems like a lifetime when silence is your only friend. Despite other members of the crew being present, the isolation was marked—despite people all around, there was no one to speak to.

When we reached London and passengers entered the plane, things seemed to gain a semblance of normalcy. Everyone wore a mask, and all you could see were their eyes. But as each passenger walked into the flight, their eyes beamed with gratitude and relief—knowing that from then on till they reached the security of their homes, they were in safe hands. I could resonate with that feeling. After flying almost all over the world, returning home at the end of a flight has been the most comforting thing. Even though I did not know the passengers personally, we developed affection and attachment for one another, the kind that comes naturally in the time of shared crisis. What was binding us in that moment was being Indian. The country and the world at large were also together in moving forward in the fight against Covid-19. We stood together to tackle what was the greatest public health challenge of a generation. Governments, healthcare workers, frontline workers (like my husband and I) were constantly working towards saving lives and minimising impact. The mission was clear. The challenge was great. Together, we were battling against 2020's very own catastrophe.

This was the first flight I'd taken since lockdown, but it was enough to reveal that the nature of flights and flying had changed drastically, almost irreparably; things were going to be very different from now on. The use of gloves and masks by flight attendants such as myself, the use of more disposables within service, a general reduction in the amount of interaction with flight crew.

The pandemic has ensured that everyone's favourite part of being on a flight—serving of the refreshments—would no longer be practised the way it used to be. All refreshments are now pre-placed in the seat pockets before passengers board. In addition to all this, passengers sitting in the middle seat have been required to wear a PPE, a head shield and of course, a mask. I came across adamant passengers who refused to follow protocols. Once, a man sitting on the aisle, refused to wear his mask and said, "Don't force me to wear a mask. I'm not likely to get Covid-19. Don't unnecessarily bother me!" I've found it best to patiently tell such passengers that they have no choice in the matter. Being careless could cost every one of us, in a big way. Earlier, people never seemed to take safety demonstrations seriously, with many passengers putting on earphones or shifting their gaze to the cabin window during them. During this time, I have had their undivided attention.

We were also yearning to go back to our families safely. For the Vande Bharat flight crew, the journey did not just end once the flight landed. There was protocol to be followed even after that. The crew had to get tested three times—before the flight, immediately after the flight, and five days after the flight. It was a tedious cycle. I felt like I was getting tested almost every second week. But those were the rules. I was grateful for the way Air India ensured the safety of their employees.

After completing three international rescue missions, I moved to domestic flights. Every passenger had their own story. Some were travelling to attend funerals of their loved ones; some were going back to reunite with their families after months of being under quarantine. There were also a couple of passengers who'd gone for a vacation and were left helpless once the lockdown was announced. The pandemic had brought about different kinds of changes in everyone's lives. It was interesting to note that even though each passenger's story and purpose of travel was different, the same fear and uncertainty shadowed everyone's faces: the cabin crew, the passenger, the pilot—all of us.

Millions of airline passengers who travelled over the holidays experienced first-hand the unsettling uncertainties that come with flying during a pandemic. The anxious glances; the awkward semi-distancing; the haphazard mask etiquette; and the absence of regular service. Soon into the newly set flying trends, an eighteen-hour flight that flew from Dubai and landed in Auckland, New Zealand, discovered evidence of an outbreak that most likely occurred during the trip. Using seat maps and genetic analysis, it was determined that one passenger initiated a chain of infection that spread to four others en route. On every flight, I say, "Your safety is our priority." Earlier, people thought it was merely lip service. This pandemic has made me put my own safety on the line to prove to everyone that their safety is, indeed, our priority. Flying was once routine. During the peak of the pandemic, it felt like a feat. Masks, health checks, even worse, detached service—long-distance travel may never be the same again. Many passengers shared with me that trips taken to destinations they are used to visiting now feel like a voyage into the unknown. They also share that booking flights was more difficult now. In efforts to redeem losses, flights often don't allow passengers to redeem online a flight voucher from a cancelled trip. Airports are emptier, more silent. After collecting their boarding passes, they walk past rows of shuttered duty-free shops. You can sometimes hear your own footsteps echoing on the polished marble tile-floor. It is strangely disquieting to travel through a deserted airport. There is no stress of standing in long queues and fighting your way through crowds.

That is just a drop in the ocean of how the coronavirus is pushing the aviation industry into new, scarier directions. Before the pandemic, airlines worried about not being able to replace retiring pilots. They were once in short supply. Now, pilots are losing their jobs. This virus has not just devastated the airline business but has also thinned the ranks of pilots by the thousands and has already put their careers on hold. The worst part right now is that the only thing we know for certain is that nobody knows anything. There's uncertainty. To prepare for that uncertain future, the world's biggest airlines are stockpiling billions in cash. Many pilot friends of mine often shared with me that "the turmoil was nerve-wrecking" for them. Unsurprisingly, pilots are passionate about their profession. That is why they spend years in gruelling training programmes, trying to rack up the minimum flight hours and credentials needed to become airline pilots.

While the pandemic has affected everyone, for me, it has been especially painful to see how these testing times have put my fellow employees under endless duress. What this meant on a personal level was a significant dent in our salaries. Despite completing over 2,000 Vande Bharat evacuations, bringing home more than 6.7 lakh Indians, crew members have had to accept 60–70 per cent cuts in their salaries. On the one hand, the nation was saluting the frontline workers with fighter jets carrying out an aerial flower shower, military bands performing at major hospitals and lighting up of warships as a way to express gratitude. But on the other, you also had salaries being cut by huge margins. There's no denying that everyone's been caught in this arduous situation. But imagine putting your blood and sweat into hours of work, away from family, the risk of catching the virus constantly hanging over your head. Wouldn't you expect to be better treated than this?

The pandemic has also wreaked havoc with jobs in the aviation sector. However, Air India being a government-owned airline was in a comparatively better position. There are two sets of employees at Air India: contractual and permanent. The former lot were constantly sceptical of whether their employment contract would be renewed or not. Permanent employees, who have provided many years of service, were on the safer side. But I could not but be aware of the havoc this pandemic had caused in the lives of people from the same industry, elsewhere. A friend of mine from Australia who was a pilot for Qantas Airlines for seventeen years had to resort to driving buses in Sydney. Many pilots and paramedics had no choice but to choose an alternative path, not knowing whether that would be a temporary or permanent fix for the problem. Their wings, growth and way of life were put on hold for the foreseeable future until the industry could stabilize and find its feet.

But on a more personal level, I was aghast by the way people were behaving with frontline workers like my husband and I. Even though the pandemic was a collective enemy, many people have responded to it in selfish ways, because for them, personal health trumps everything else. The fact that the virus is contagious has rendered everyone extremely critical of others' behaviours.

When I first started to fly with the Vande Bharat crew, my neighbours would often give me disapproving looks, as if saying, "Why is she stepping out during a pandemic?" People failed to—sometimes refused to—understand that it wasn't a personal choice. It was my job. The store I went to buy groceries from refused to sell to our household. Even though my children had no role to play in my decision to fly, they had to bear the brunt of it. Neighbours consciously reduced their conversation with us and would even avoid greeting us. It felt extremely discouraging to be receiving such treatment for no fault of mine.

Over time, however, I did see their questionable gazes turn into admiration. Once frontline workers worldwide began to be appreciated on social media and on national television, the "why do you need to step out and put us all at risk?" became "we're so proud of what you're doing". These words meant a lot to me;

watching other frontline workers—doctors, nurses, journalists, police officers, et al—going on tirelessly kept me motivated. The pandemic brought us together by fate in an ominous sort of way, but what we have made of it is truly inspiring. Our collective empathy, gratitude and patience have seen us through these tough times. In all my interactions, I always found less to criticise and more to appreciate.

Many flight attendants were grounded for months, especially those who work in private airlines. While the future of travel and aviation at large remains uncertain, some of my closest, long-time friends in the industry are considering giving up a career that provided them stable income, constant adventure and had become a way of life. As flight attendants, we take on various roles in the public imagination, as part of our job: we are a nurse when a passenger is unwell, a companion in the skies for those travelling alone, a doting provider for anything a traveller requires—all of this while looking glamorous. However, it's hard not to appreciate the perks: the moment when the sun shines in through the airplane window, schedule flexibility, international travel and more. It gives you perspective on how you want to spend your working hours and your life. However, that view became out of reach for many of us. With millions of employees being furloughed, it was anything but a stable career anymore. Some of us (including me) planned to do this forever. Our role goes beyond conducting the safety demonstrations and serving refreshments. We are there for people in their good times and bad times. Be it to reassure passengers if they are afraid of turbulence or to share the excitement when little kids experience flying for the first time or be it wishing people who are going to reunite with their loved ones, well. But in the recent months, we've only seen the social world of this profession shrink.

For some of my friends, their last flight before the lockdown was their last flight as an attendant—and they had no clue. They are at a stage in their career (forty years or more) when it is difficult to make a switch. Working as a frontline worker means you have spent your entire life training to be a good fit for that one position. If you are in that job, chances are, that is all you've ever wanted to do. In some cases, their families depend on them. The pandemic took away their life and livelihood, all at once—without any warning.

This is far from a traditional nine-to-five office job. There are delays, exhaustion. You miss special family events. There are sacrifices. At the same time, our office is a beautiful sky with white puffy clouds. Flying in a pandemic definitely introduced new challenges to an already demanding job. But that's what we're taught in our training—how to de-escalate a situation. Take a tense situation and make it survivable. So, that's what we did and will continue to do until the world is in a better place. Those of us who have been in the profession for a while have come to expect this. You kind of know going in that aviation has its high highs and low lows. You do it because you love what you do.

5

A Generation Bookended by Tragedies

Suditi Sundaram, High School Student, Class 12

Editors' Note

Energy-draining virtual classes, the need to focus on studies amidst worries about repaying loans, postponed internships, difficult career decisions, the stress of finding a job in the midst of a lockdown when your health is at risk and your loved ones are falling sick—the peak of the coronavirus pandemic was extremely hard-hitting for college students, as it did for students across the spectrum. It fundamentally altered what they desired from their jobs and lives, like it did for many of us.

Covid-19 created a situation that simultaneously threatened both the economy and public health. College students too were overwhelmed by this threat and faced an acute crisis. In addition to feelings of loneliness, fragile career expectations, managing the day-to-day stress of the situation, they were also dealing with a major life transition—graduating from college to seeking a job.

However, Gen Z is well known for its ability to adapt. As more and more things began getting cancelled during the lockdown, and there was increasing uncertainty about the future, they started appreciating things they took for granted. It's surprising, almost inspiring, that some students in the graduating classes of 2020 were still filled with hope during the time. They took the time to reflect on and accept the current situation, which put them in a better position to manage their goals in an uncertain world.

*

We are the generation that was born after 9/11 and entered adulthood in the middle of a pandemic. We are a generation bookended by tragedies.

Most of us were born not long after the 11 September 2001 terrorist attacks, a day that scrambled all notions of predictability. News surrounding natural calamities, cyber-attack, harassment, racial discrimination and more, dominated the television we grew up watching. News for us was no longer a source of information but rather something that instigated a strong sense of pessimism. This is also when we were introduced to social media, a phenomenon we literally grew up with. We were young when history got its first African–American president, still young when another history-making president was sworn in. And then came Covid-19, the news of which felt personal. It felt as though we will be remembered as the class that didn't get to do any "exciting" stuff because of coronavirus. Sometimes I wondered if we would be remembered as "the Corona Class".

As an army kid, changing schools, making new friends, adapting to a new environment and constantly being on the move has been a part and parcel of life. I've changed nearly twelve schools, studied in international as well as national schools, and completed classes 10, 11 and 12 from three different schools. I've never had a place that I could call home. In fact, whenever someone asks me, "Where are you from?",

I instantly smirk and ramble on for half an hour addressing why I don't have a definitive answer to that question. Having a group of "childhood" friends, growing up next to the same neighbours or having the same schoolteachers throughout your schooling were some experiences I never had. But despite all the turbulence experienced in my schooling up until this point, I wouldn't say I suffered. I embraced the newness with each new atmosphere and built a comfort zone for myself there. I had a choice. I could choose my subjects, who I would become friends with, what sport I played, etc.

But little did I know what lay ahead of me.

It was a day in March. I was sitting in the canteen of my school, an international baccalaureate school in Qatar, with my friends, waiting for our next lecture to begin. One of our teachers walked in and started to usher students out of the school premises, informing us that the school would be shutting down. At the time, it felt like a mere drill, something that would normalise in a week's time. I asked a friend, "Do you want to come over to my house?" We took the bus home. We cooked together and watched a movie that was trending on Netflix at the time.

Our new life started to become clear to us not long after, when I checked in with my friend about plans to meet for lunch. She responded, "My parents just read an article about social distancing and are not allowing any get-togethers." That was it. That bland afternoon of cooking together was the last memorable event of my last year in school. The filling of forms for graduation, prom, senior day signing, the house parties, the mindless banter between classes—all of it was lost to the lockdown.

Instagram was all we had from now on. Classmates, seniors and friends from other schools would often post images of studying-from-home, of missing school, of being extremely bored or lonely. I would relate to it and often text them sharing the same. Some of my friends were dating or were involved in serious relationships that they hoped would continue into their college lives. They were anxious that the pandemic would put those relationships in jeopardy. Some others had been very excited about all the crazy things they would do when they passed out from school, some were curious about the girls they'd meet in college, some about finally having a hostel room, and others about getting jobs to support their parents.

Soon, these conversations started turning around. They became about how miserable online graduation would make us feel, how they were tired of sharing a room with their sibling, or how they needed to get jobs to support their parents who had been laid off. I, personally, was looking forward to resting at home for a little bit. Despite all the emotions, I doubt that all of us had realised the magnitude of the situation at the outset. Initially, it felt like an adventure. A staycation.

Soon after, the gravity of the situation with regard to the coronavirus started flashing on daily news. The economy fell apart. Families faltered. People died by the millions. For us, however, school was down to its final months. Our teachers had talked about a virus that was causing lockdowns and death on the other side of the world, but now it was here. It was everywhere.

After years of cliques and grudges, awkward phases and social mishaps—the end of high school was beginning to provide a *Breakfast Club* moral to the story: everyone realising they have been in this together. You know that classic scene in *Mean Girls*? How all the different cliques have different tables? It took until this year for everybody to get their heads screwed on a bit straighter. It's like, "Why would you continue beefing about people when you're not going to see them after this year?"

We are starting to see that having social interaction in person and in the flesh is significant, and I don't think we are going to take that for granted anymore.

I think this is why seniors cry at their graduations. And it is what made the situation especially difficult for our class. The coronavirus had destroyed all traditions: the all-encompassing paranoia before exams, the thrill of finding the perfect outfit for farewell and being engulfed with the sorrow of saying final goodbyes.

While there were emotional and psychological consequences of these unfortunate circumstances, there were some academic ones as well. One afternoon, in the middle of this pandemic, came more bad news. Two life-altering emails. One read that the final exams—those that would have defined our future—stand cancelled. The second one read, "…we are regretful to inform you that the official graduation ceremony will now take place over video conferencing." Let's deal with the first one first.

Here's some information that may interest you: while studying the International Baccalaureate program, 20 per cent of one's final grade depends on internal assessments (IAs) and 80 per cent on the final exam. Understandably, one invests time and effort in both accordingly, but none of us were aware or could even fathom the cancellation of our final International Baccalaureate Diploma Programme (IBDP) exams. We entertained the possibility of them getting postponed. But cancelled? That was something no one was prepared for. I'd personally been working extremely hard for the final exams as 80 per cent of my grade depended on it. Now, that 80 per cent was down to zero. I spiralled into a chain of worrying questions: were my IAs and other class assignments good enough? What if I fail? Will I not get into a university of my choice? What if I disappoint my parents?

The email might as well have read, "100 per cent of your grade has already been accounted for; in case of any errors, there is no opportunity for redemption." A few weeks later, we received our final grades. There was approximately a 7–8 point drop from what our teachers had predicted we would get. (Fun Fact: Predicted scores are also sent to universities, on the basis of which, they give you admission.) Thankfully for me, I had an unconditional university offer letter in hand, but I felt terrible for friends who didn't. My friends reached out to me expressing how helpless, scared and worried they were.

*

Globally, there was a huge drop in the final scores received by IB students across the world. A global petition was signed by nearly 7,000 people in the initial days after the results were out, highlighting the agony faced by students and parents alike. Social media was flooded with anxious posts regarding university admissions.

In India, the Central Board of Secondary Education (CBSE), which is the national-level board of education in the country, also cancelled the board exams for classes 10 and 12, which are considered crucial for university admissions. It was declared that the final assessment would be done on the basis of internal assessments, or on the basis of marks scored in the pre-board examinations. Contrary to the IB results, the overall pass percentage for CBSE Class 12 exams in 2020 saw an increase from the previous year. The percentage in 2020 was 88.78 per cent compared to 83.40 per cent in 2019. In addition, considering the mental health turmoil the students would be facing during the times of crisis, CBSE also replaced the term "Fail" in the marksheets with "Essential Repeat".

*

Some of my friends had signed up for internships abroad, all of which were now cancelled. A few students from my school were immediately called back to their home country in the middle of completing their semester abroad. All of our dreams and aspirations were now a huge question mark. This period was supposed to be the time where we transition from teenagers to young adults and start to "figure stuff out" on our own but what kind of a start was this?

Some students were persuaded to apply for re-evaluation of their marks, while some accepted the misfortune brought upon by the pandemic and decided to move on. I fell in the latter half. I didn't have the strength to fight.

Just a week prior, I had so much to look forward to and now, I had lost it all. We, as a class, were eagerly looking forward to our graduation ceremony. At this point, all we were asking was, "What is it that we lost?" It was so hard to grasp the loss of something that did not even happen for us. The love that rains from the bleachers, the energy of the last gathering of one-time strangers who became a class. The calling of the name. The handshake on the stage. The farewell to one's childhood. I emailed a few teachers and friends who had made an impression on me in my years at school. As far as meeting in person went, Covid-19 had effectively closed doors to those possibilities.

Our graduation ceremony took place virtually. The faculty and other organisers did their best to make it seem as personal and close to the in-person ceremony as possible. The class of 2020 was finally together in spirit but scattered across the globe, celebrating this monumental point in our lives. But, on a screen. Although one couldn't oversee the physical limitations, what was beautiful was that emotionally, everyone felt more connected as a community than ever. There was a conscious awareness of what each of us was going through that made the ceremony feel more special.

The ceremony began with an address by the head of school. Four minutes into his speech, tears started rolling down my eyes and as I glanced on my screen, I could see more people crying and reaching out for tissues. His words of empathy did restore hope. Hope for us to bounce back, better and stronger. The address was followed by a video compilation of senior year. Pictures from our school trip, annual events at school, plays and sports day played one after the other. I relived my senior year in that five-minute video. It reminded me of just how happy I was in those moments and I felt nothing but gratitude for having made such memories in the first place. All in all, while I was apprehensive about having an online graduation ceremony, by the end of it, I couldn't have been gladder that it happened. It was a reminder of all the things I had worked for, achieved and a push to do better going forward.

The coronavirus has stripped students, across the world, of the milestones that traditionally signal the transition to adulthood. We are the largest student population in history to have shifted overnight from our brick-and-mortar classroom to virtual classrooms, adapting to an entirely different way of learning on the fly. As high-school graduates, we feel as though it is our responsibility to strive to become a generation of medical researchers who develop cures and vaccines, or elected officials who put laws and policies in place so that we're better prepared to help prevent a future pandemic. We can, and should, be the corporate leaders who empathise with parents who have to work remotely. The engineers who build technology tools and platforms for online learning. However, for many of us, those dreams look bleak and unattainable. Many of my friends were admitted into colleges abroad, based on the scores we were predicted to accomplish. A "conditional admission" as it's widely known. However, due to the gaps in online learning and many other mental stresses Covid-19 brought along with it, they were unable to meet those scores. Those who applied to college in many European countries and were unable to meet their predicted scores, dropped a year and reapplied with better scores. In the US and UK, however, universities are lowering expectations in wake of Covid-19.

*

University of Birmingham was among the first few universities to have reduced its entry/admission requirements for most of its undergraduate programmes by one grade. Many universities, under the Russell Group, saw a high number of vacancies on approximately 4,000 courses. These include traditionally sought-after courses such as law, engineering and English literature. This led to their decision of lifting student number controls, meaning that universities can recruit as many undergraduates as they see fit.

In India, the Indian Institutes of Technology (IITs) around the country are the most prestigious institutions when it comes to research and development in science, engineering and technology. In a first-ever move, the universities decided to drop the minimum requirement of a score of 75 per cent in Class 12 for the academic year due to the pandemic and instead only demanded a passing certificate.

For those already in university and moving towards the job pool, the situation was completely different. Way worse, in many ways. Some of them have seen their parents being laid off, losing jobs or closing businesses—and that forced some students to jump in earlier than planned to help their families financially. And that has, in turn, compelled them to take a long, hard look at their personal ambitions. Was what they originally intended to do after graduation still worth it?

Additionally, many areas they'd hoped to secure jobs in no longer offered positions. Law offices, fashion brands and others have cancelled internships and postponed interviews. Students have had to wander through empty job fairs and live through recruiters ignoring their anxious emails. Their entry was into a job market grimmer than any in recent history. All jobs or career ideas of seniors in college stood upended. Suddenly, they were left looking into a void.

*

By this time, we were ready to attend college—online. All my expectations, the things that I saw my elder sister experience, those that I'd viewed in movies, those that I'd daydreamed about, were all shattered. I felt cheated. College is where you are supposed to be getting a fresh new start. High school is done, and you are no longer being babied. But now, as reality dawned, college was on a screen. In my opinion, there may be no demographic as ill-equipped for isolation as students who are about to enter college. I mean, we have hormones, for crying out loud. We were all buzzing with energy. Sports teams, best friends, new relationships, going to the mall before our freshers' party— social contact was an essential part of being a teenager.

And yet isolation had been thrust upon us.

It has been a year since online classes began but I feel so used to them now. It's the same drill: me locked in my study room, glued to my screen, speaking to faces behind my laptop that I would have otherwise interacted with in person. It's hard. It's hard to deliver the same concentration, focus and interest that one could deliver in a physical classroom. There is a reason for designated study environments in universities and schools as they steer the required academic vigour.

More than an excitement about learning something new each day, online classes became just another mundane task. The energy I had in the first couple of weeks began fading as days progressed. I had classmates who would join the class, turn off their video and microphone and go back to sleep. Since there was no way of keeping a check on whether students were actually present, students took advantage and missed classes.

Online classes also restricted the scope of relationship between a professor and a student. Due to the impersonal medium of communication, the question of approaching the professor outside of class did not arise. In normal circumstances, you could always catch them later in college or head to their cabin during lunch or schedule a meeting post working hours. That wasn't the case now. Majority of the interaction between with professors was limited to the one-and-a-half-hour zoom call. One cannot blame them either. They were in the process of adapting to this new method of learning themselves and had their own share of challenges. Apart from classes, the inductions for all clubs and societies also happened online. We had to submit online application forms and auditions to be considered in various clubs. Our official fresher's party got postponed to when our batch would be present on campus.

However, by the end of December 2020 and early January 2021, things seemed to finally be in control. India was recording very few numbers of Covid-19 cases and our university had permitted students to return to campus. I immediately filled out my campus return application form and eagerly awaited a response from the university. Within ten days, I got an email that read, "Campus request application approved." It was the first time in a year where I felt immense joy. I'd already lost six months of my college life but now I had a chance to make up for the lost time. In this period, through online classes and virtual interactions, I'd made many friends at the university and I couldn't wait to finally meet them. I quickly packed all my stuff, reached campus and started settling in. But as luck would have it, just within twenty days of us being in college, being independent and living the typical college life, things changed. Again.

Covid-19 was back and this time, it was worse. The second wave of the coronavirus left the country in tatters. The exponential growth in Covid-19 cases and an anticipation of another lockdown led our dean to request students to head back home. I had to pack everything once again and within a couple of hours, I was back home. It felt like I was watching a movie and it had ended abruptly. The twenty days I spent at university felt surreal. Did they even happen? I was home again and this time, till August. In essence, I'd lost my entire first year of college. It wasn't just me though. Schools and colleges in various parts of India declared early summer vacations, IGCSE and CBSE cancelled their board exams and everything that happened in 2020 was happening once again. I don't think I can even put into words how I felt. It wasn't so black and white anymore. We were living through extreme personal and, at some level, a collective anguish. At a personal level, through suspended relationships and disrupted college plans, Covid-19 has altered us, disrupted us, redirected us. At the global level, the resounding tremors have been of a seismic kind. It may yet define us.

Yet, we are the class of 2020 with that perfect vision. We do know how to make our lives better. During every dark time across history, people rise and cope—more than cope really. They demonstrate resilience, creativity and an ability to innovate. We came up with the #Coronavirussyllabus which developed, as many things do these days, on Twitter. Through this hashtag, widely used by teachers across the world, we tried to capture all the ways human society has tried and is trying to make sense of this quite dramatic change. In America, they closed the Wi-Fi gap using school buses. Yes, it is exactly what it sounds like. They turned school buses into Wi-Fi hotspots to help low-income and rural areas with access to high-speed internet so they can continue to learn from home.

The global pandemic may have robbed us of some of the most defining moments of our lives, but it has also given us a lot to cherish. More than anything else, it has reaffirmed our faith in the fact that we can get through our darkest hours, together as a generation.

6

Whose Country Is It Anyway?

A Migrant Worker from Bihar

Editors' Note

India has one of the world's largest homeless populations, and the lockdown swelled these numbers exponentially. Approximately 80 per cent of India's 470 million workers are in the informal sector (the portion of a country's economy that lies outside of any formal regulatory environment). Informal sector activities are rarely reflected in official statistics on economic activity (for example, gross domestic product). At least 45 million of these come from the countryside, according to government estimates.

While a nationwide lockdown may have come as a mere inconvenience to a large part of the Indian population, it proved to be a humanitarian crisis for the rest. According to official data, over 2.6 million migrant workers were stranded across the country, with no source of income or means to return to their hometowns. Where safety was paramount, it was not affordable to many. With no option left, men, women and children began walking on foot on empty roads with heavy luggage under the scorching April sun. When asked about their destinations, their answers ranged from

Bihar, Uttar Pradesh, Jharkhand and various other states that they called "home", thousands of kilometres away. According to the 2001 census, more than 50 per cent migrants to Delhi/NCR come from Bihar and Uttar Pradesh. During 1991–2001, the percentage share of migration from Bihar increased from 5.77 per cent to 19.09 per cent.

Some could make it back home and some could not. Many succumbed to the unfavourable weather conditions, while many met with accidents along the way. Due to the lack of data on the death of migrant workers, there was no compensation provided to the families. Looking at the migrant worker exodus, the only question on everyone's minds was: why isn't anyone doing anything about this situation? In May 2020, the government sprang into action and announced Shramik special trains to carry migrant workers back home. Of the 3,740 Shramik trains that ran since 1 May, about 40 per cent were recorded as late. The average delay was about eight hours, with 421 trains delayed by about ten hours; some 373 running late by up to twenty-four hours; almost seventy-eight trains delayed by over twenty-four hours; forty-three trains late by thirty hours or more; and a few by two days or more. Most of the delayed trains were bound for Bihar and Uttar Pradesh.

Around 17 May 2020, a little over a month into the lockdown, a construction worker in Delhi made headlines. Rampukar Pandit became representative of India's migrant worker tragedy. A photograph of him sobbing by a road in Delhi led to a huge dialogue—a depiction of the grim realities of being a migrant worker in India. The cause of his misery was his dying son back in Bihar. He was anguished at the thought that he might not make it home in time to see his baby boy, who was just a few months old. He pleaded to the police to understand his situation, to make an exception, to let him go home and hold his new-born baby at least once. To which, the policemen replied, "Will your son suddenly come alive if you go back home? This is a serious matter—larger than your personal sob story. You cannot and will not move."

"We labourers have no life; we are just a cog in the wheel, spinning continuously until we run out of life," the thirty-eight-year-old Rampukar Pandit shared with one of India's leading newspapers, The Hindu. *Fortunately, a woman from Delhi and a photographer (the one who clicked the viral snapshot) saved him. The woman gave him food, Rs 550 and booked his ticket. "The rich will get all the help they need, in situations that are far less intense than this. They're getting rescued and being brought back home in planes from abroad. But workers and labourers like us have been left to fend for ourselves. That is the worth of our lives.* Hum mazdooron ka koi desh nahin hota *(we labourers don't belong to any country)," he shared.*

News channels showed grim images of migrant workers walking under the scorching heat of Indian summer. Some had been asked to leave by their landlords; some were desperate because of monetary constraints. There were plenty of reasons, but it all came down to one thing: they had no choice. Those with money and houses could stay locked in, survive on savings. They could work from home and still earn some money. But for the migrant workers, that was not a possibility.

Speaking about the plight of migrant workers during the lockdown and whether "thousands of migrant labourers have died during lockdown", the minister of state for labour and employment replied that "no such data is available".

The future of migrant workers, their livelihood and work remain a huge question mark. Most of them have had to start from scratch. The life and routine built over decades were uprooted as a result of the pandemic. Income, livelihood, family stability, had all been lost. Therefore, after their return home, they had to look for new viable sources of income, a place to live, ways to settle the family, all with no external aid.

Post the inconvenient journey to their respective villages, the return of migrant workers back to cities remains uncertain. Some, aware of the "dispensable and cheap" nature of their labour, are afraid to risk and take the plunge of returning. Only questions loom over their heads: Will their work resume? Will their wages see a massive hit? What is the guarantee that they will not be faced with such a precarious situation again?

However, the same cities and employers who turned their backs on the workers when the lockdown was announced wanted them back after it was lifted. The demand for labourers soared. Therefore, there are also a chunk of workers who are ready to embrace the risks at the cost of being exploited as, at the end of the day, it comes down to feeding the belly.

At the same time, the disruption to supply chains and closed borders resulting from the pandemic has also pushed firms to adapt to technology and automation. This shift may come as bad news for migrant workers as technology would act as a substitute for physical labour.

Rajesh (name changed) is one such face in the crowd of thousands who struggled to return home. His narrative offers insights into his mental, physical and psychological state during that time. This is a story that humanises the numbers we constantly read or heard about.

*

"Ye desh aakhir kiska hai? Unchi buildingon mein rehene walon ka ya un buildingon ki buniyaad ko banane wale mazdooron ka?" (Who does the country belong to? Does it belong to those living in high-rise buildings or to the labourers who built the very foundations of those buildings?)

I am a migrant worker. I have a wife and two children—a twelve-year-old daughter and a thirty-year-old son. Very early on in life, I'd understood the importance and value of money. *Paisa nahi toh kuch nahi* (If you don't have money, you have nothing). I had also understood the role education plays in determining a person's standing in the world. I was determined to go to school, determined to break the curse poverty brings with it. By picking up menial jobs such as sweeping and washing laundry as a dhobi in my village, I managed to save enough money to get me through to high school. Then, reality kicked in. My family members wanted my monetary support. Hence, the ambition of education remained incomplete.

I was told by my uncle who worked in Delhi that if I wanted to earn money, I should look for a way to move out of the village. He suggested that I shift to a metropolitan city which could provide stability, higher income and a better standard of living. Considering the benefits of this move, I along with my wife and children moved from our hometown, Jamalpur in Bihar, and came to Noida. My uncle spoke to a building contractor in Noida and requested him to offer me a job.

I was going to get paid Rs 560 per day. Compared to how much I was getting paid in Bihar, Rs 450 per day, this was a considerable increase. I then persuaded my wife to join me since the contribution from her additional work would ensure more income. When you earn barely Rs 400 a day, and have to eat, run a household, send your kids to school, prioritising education isn't even an option. The cash in your hand disappears in no time.

Soon after settling down in Noida, my wife and I started working for the building contractor. The two of us would go to work at the construction site every morning, and our kids would go to a local government school in our neighbourhood.

There were difficulties, but we had a decent life. *Jaise bhi ho, hum khushi se guzaara kar rahe the* (Somehow, we were managing to get by and live happily). My son is happily married with a family of his own now.

In 2020, around early March, I started hearing about the coronavirus on news channels, on radio shows, from the people I'd meet at our *chai tapri* (tea stall); even from bade sahib, my boss. I didn't really understand what it was back then—people were being asked to wear face masks, constantly wash their hands, and keep their distance from one another. *Koi bimaari thi jo Cheen se aayi thi* (it was some disease that came from China). Everyone seemed to have something to say about it. But whatever it was, it had shaken the world and stirred everything up. People were terrified of getting sick.

In our family, we were more concerned about making ends meet. That is the reality of daily wage earners. We didn't pay much thought to this new disease, and life went on as usual.

On 25 March, my wife and I went to work like any other day. But when we reached the site, we could hardly see anyone around. Usually, the area would have nearly a hundred or so workers. On this day, there were only six or seven people—all standing around, looking confused, just like us. I turned to one of the workers in the group, "*Kya ho raha hai? Sab log kahan hai?*" (What is happening? Where is everyone?). He looked at me grimly and replied, "*Bhai, poore desh mein lockdown bol diya gaya hai. Modi-ji ne TV pe bola hai. Ab se yahan kaam nahi hone wala. Humein bol rahe hain ki yahan se chale jao.*" (The whole nation is under lockdown. Modi-ji announced it on the TV. No work is going to happen here from now on. They're asking us to leave.)

I was worried, but I thought it would be over soon. Only a few days back a Janata Curfew was announced, and that lasted less than a day. How bad could it be?

When we returned home, we learnt more about this lockdown. Twenty-one days of lockdown—to fight the virus.

What I heard was—twenty-one days of no work, no *money*. I, and everyone around me—migrant workers especially—was taking up any work that would help them make money on a day-to-day basis. Plumbing, construction, rag-picking, loading and unloading goods, and other laborious tasks. Staying at home was a luxury we couldn't afford.

On the twenty-first day, we were told that the lockdown had been extended further. Already struggling to get by, having run out of whatever little we had saved up to feed ourselves, this news came as a heavy blow. Before, we had held on because there was a light at the end of the tunnel. Now, no one knew. With no money coming in, how would I arrange food for my wife, my daughter and myself? The only savings we had now was for my daughter's wedding.

I was confused and scared. The people I used to work with were planning to return to their hometowns. There was no work here. There seemed to be no reliable information on when the lockdown would be lifted. It made sense to go back home. Without earning, none of us could sustain the cost of living in the capital.

But one question burned in our minds: How will we go?

All transportation had been suspended. Buses and trains were all we could afford, but they were no longer running. No emergency transportation had been arranged for us; we didn't even get enough time to make any plans. *Hum taiyaariyan karte toh kab*? (When could we have made arrangements?) Sanjeev Bhai said, "*Ek hi raasta hai. Paidal nikalna padega.*" (There is only one option. We'll have to walk on foot.)

The very next morning, Sanjeev Bhai and his family had packed up their belongings along with six bottles of water, blankets, rugs and some rotis and achaar for the way. I went to say goodbye, not knowing when I would see him and Bhabhi again.

"*Kab tak pahunchoge Jaunpur*?" (By when do you think you'll reach Jaunpur?)

Jaunpur is Sanjeev's hometown.

"*Bhai, pata nahi. Kuch hafte toh araam se lag jayenge*." (I don't know. But it will easily take a couple of weeks.)

I wished Sanjeev Bhai well. I desperately wanted to head back to my hometown too, but I couldn't risk the health of my wife and child. How would my forty-five-year-old wife and twelve-year-old girl walk all the way back to Bihar?

Twelve days after Sanjeev Bhai's departure, I wondered how far they had reached. But when I tried calling his number, it was switched off. Maybe he had turned it off to save the battery? Or maybe it had already run out of battery, and he had no way of communicating? I prayed for his good health every day, wondering where he was, how he and Bhabhi were managing.

*

This mass reverse migration began April–May 2020, and without proper arrangements for transport, many started their journey back home on foot, cycles, or by hitching rides. By early June, close to 200 migrant workers had died in road accidents. Migrant workers, killed during their efforts to go back home, comprised 26.4 per cent of the overall deaths during the lockdown, with UP accounting for over 30 per cent of the total deaths.

*

With businesses shut down in cities across the country, we saw vast numbers of other migrants—many of whom (like us) lived and ate at the site of their work—who were suddenly without food and shelter. More than a dozen migrant labourers (some of them are friends) lost their lives, as they tried to return to their home. Thousands of migrants, including whole families packed their pots, pans and blankets into rucksacks, which they had to carry along, some also balancing their children on their shoulders as they walked along interstate highways. Some planned to walk hundreds of miles. But as they reached the Delhi border, many were beaten back by the police. It felt as if the entire nation feared the disease, but we feared hunger more.

I was not afraid of getting the virus. I was not afraid of dying. Living in such extreme, hopeless conditions was already killing us in a way. Each day, I saw more and more people heading home—on cycles, on rickshaws, by foot.

In the absence of a clear policy, we were left to the whims of the police. There were instances where we were treated inhumanely. "Leave this place! Go inside. Separate! Separate! Maintain distance!" they would yell through their loudspeakers. When the situation went beyond their verbal control, they resorted to beating us with bamboo sticks. Usually, the country's array of religious institutions—temples, gurdwaras and mosques—would come to our rescue when we were extremely hungry. But now, everything was closed.

When the lockdown was announced, I saw those who had the money buy lots and lots of food items—hoarding essentials that would last them months. What about those dying from hunger? We could only plan one meal at a time. With each passing day, my despair mounted. My savings and willpower continued to run out and there seemed to be no end to this in sight. I had to do something. It had already been more than a month since we'd been idle at home. How long could this continue? I asked my son if we could live with him for a few days; this was our only option if we wanted to sustain for long. He hesitated—he has his own family to think of—but agreed. He told us that he too was facing a crunch and wouldn't be able to help out much. I didn't mind; every bit counted in such times.

But eight days in, I had a fallout with my son. He asked us to leave immediately. He said that there was no place for us; we were only adding to his problems.

Turned away from the last source of hope, we set out again—this time heading straight to the railway station. In the first week of May, the government had announced that over 4,000 Shramik Special trains were to be employed to take migrant workers back to their hometowns.

While the news of these trains came as a huge relief, what also accompanied it was the assumption that the Shramik Special trains were responsible for the spread of Covid-19 throughout India. This myth was extremely frustrating and difficult to deal with. The lockdown just failed to contain the spread of the coronavirus—they were blaming the trains, because they were afraid to take the blame for a mistake they had made. Hence, the blame for the spread of the nation's deadliest virus was on us. I watched the news on my phone. Many reporters argued that we were taking the virus, hitherto concentrated in the cities, to rural areas and to "almost every corner" of the country. It proliferated rapidly in the trains and unleashed devastation. An international news magazine called the Shramik Special, the "Virus Trains". This is nothing but the entrenched prejudices that resulted in bleach being sprayed on us to sanitise us, police brutally beating us up and dehumanising us.

*

The data simply didn't add up. Most of these reports followed a similar pattern: they were based on ground reports from one or two districts and the situation in these districts was generalised. This is a classic case of sampling bias. These reports also note that a significant number of confirmed infections in many districts were of migrant workers who had just returned from elsewhere. However, it is also important to note that none of these reports state the number of tests that were actually conducted on returning migrants—in comparison to the total tests being conducted in those districts. Additionally, three states—Uttar Pradesh, Bihar and Jharkhand—accounted for the highest number of Shramik Special trains, about 75 per cent of the total trains run, until May. However, nearly four out of every five districts in these three states had detected infections even before the first Shramik train reached its destination. The reality is far from the narrative. While a portion of the returning migrant workers may have carried the virus along with them, there isn't enough data to prove that their journey back home was the reason for the spread of Covid-19 across the country.

*

I had no clue about the train timings, whether I needed a ticket or not, how much it would cost. I just knew we had to get home. I told my wife, "*Yahaan hamara kuch nahi bacha*" (There is nothing left for us here.)

A few people told me that the Shramik Specials were functioning from the railway station at Dadri. Hoping to get one step closer home, we made our way to Dadri in an auto. After about an hour, we reached the railway station. I could see around forty people sitting outside the station with their belongings. A voice on the loudspeaker said that the next train was heading towards Aurangabad and would depart at 8 p.m. It was 2 p.m., and we had to go to Bihar. I went to a police official to ask about the train that would take us back to our hometown. He seemed just as clueless as I was.

"*Yahan baithe rahiye. Jab humein pata chalega train ke baare mein, hum aapko bata denge*" (Just sit here. When we have information about your train, we'll let you know). When I told my wife exactly what the police official had said to me, I watched the hope leave her eyes.

The sun was scorching. There was no sign of shade around. But at least we were not the only ones in this plight. The platform was thronging with people waiting for something to take them home. Tired from all the travelling, my daughter rested her head against our suitcase and shut her eyes. Three hours had gone by and there was still no news. I went to a kirana shop near the station to buy some water and a packet of biscuits. We hadn't eaten since the morning; even hunger had faded by now. I spoke to a few others around me, asking about their destination, how long they'd been sitting there, etc. Some people had been waiting here for two or three days already.

Eventually, I made peace with the fact that it was all up to destiny now. I lay down in a corner of the station, with my bag cushioning my head. I thought to myself, "*Ek ameer ki shikayatein iss waqt meri aashayein bann kar reh jayengi. Usey apne ghar par rehene se shikayat hai, aur mujhe apne ghar pohonchne ki iccha hai.*" (At this moment, a rich person's complaint would be my desire. They complain about having to stay at their house, and I only want to get back to mine.)

As I lay there, I realised that in all the chaos and desperation, I had not said goodbye to the house that had become our home over the last few years. I am from Bihar, but a huge part of me was also in Noida. And now I was leaving one, with no idea when or if I'd be coming back, as I was headed to the other with no path in sight.

We waited for almost two days. Finally, I heard an announcement calling people to board the train for Bihar. A full-fledged screening took place before we were allowed inside. Officials checked our temperature to see if we showed any symptoms of the virus or not, the trains were fully disinfected and sanitised, and we were given small packages of food for the journey. For the majority of people outside, not getting infected was the ultimate priority, but for the thousands of us on this train, getting back home was all that mattered, even if it meant getting infected. For us, the coronavirus was only a mild threat. Hunger, heat, exhaustion ... there were a hundred things that could kill us before the virus.

As we settled down and the train set off, I heaved a sigh of relief. But quietly, I wondered how many were still left behind—waiting at the station, waiting to go back home. Would their trains ever arrive?

7

It's All About the Pivot

Rohan Mirchandani, CEO and Co-founder, Epigamia

Editors' Note

Many businesses and some giant corporations have been casualties of the pandemic. Not many say it, but being an entrepreneur can get lonely. It includes a lot of emotions. Going through a downturn and making tough decisions to keep your company afloat is hard. It's like going back to when you first started. However, business owners (especially of small- or medium-sized businesses) are great at staying nimble. It's something they've been set up to do because they've always had to deal with adversity in some way.

With the coronavirus restrictions, entrepreneurs were learning in real time just how they needed to adapt to survive. Business owners across the world were looking for ways to survive the pandemic, adapting business models and innovating products so that they and their employees could get back to work. However, they understood that even though they were looking to do new, innovative things to survive, they needed to grow where they had planted—they could not completely change what they did, but had to find new ways to deliver their product, dust off old ideas, experiment with existing strengths, search for new customers or change the way they told their story. Some businesses also found themselves in a position where they could help fight the pandemic. Others started searching high and low for new customers.

Among other obstacles, employers have developed bittersweet relationships with their employees. Due to the insurmountable workload and indefinite work hours topped with the disconnect caused by virtual conferencing, it has been hard to keep up healthy relationships to say the least. However, those who still lead with compassion continued to touch the lives of their employees in an extraordinary way and have probably come out of the slowdown stronger than ever before, enhancing the shared values of their staff.

This is the story of how a compassionate and intelligent entrepreneur pivoted his business in the face of the coronavirus pandemic.

*

We may have seen the end of the corporate office as we knew it. In my line of work, it is important to adapt fast. In the face of catastrophic market environments, "speed" takes on another meaning. Running a business during the Covid-19 crisis has meant making key adjustments to the way we conduct daily tasks, and at times, reconsidering our approach entirely. If things work out, we do get to receive accolades but when situations take a turn for the worse, we also have to bear the brunt. Either way, we are accountable. Especially when facing a precarious market where there is great uncertainty about the future of consumer products, the only choice is to stay armed and cross the bridge when it comes. As an entrepreneur, for better or for worse, it is almost second nature to me to inculcate flexibility in approach as a way to adapt to unpredictable business environments. All of this, while still struggling to keep the dream alive.

I've typically had an active lifestyle: alternating between home and work fronts, which has meant spending a couple of months in India with my team at Epigamia, before returning to my wife and kids back home in the United States for a few weeks. Thus, the very notion of being stuck in one place initially seemed untenable. When the lockdown was first announced, I was in New York, beginning a three-week pause to visit my family. By then, the crisis had taken global proportions, and New York was incidentally one of the epicentres of the spread. At the time, the goal was to return to India as soon as circumstances would permit; however, the more pressing concern was to temporarily move out of NY to a safer alternative location. My wife and sons, along with my parents, brother, sister-in-law and their children soon thereafter moved to a house in Delaware, where we spent the rest of the lockdown.

During the early days, the time zone difference with India made it complicated to divide my time between work and home commitments, and overall demanded a lot of patience and adjusting. Even today, I am not entirely certain about my work hours or sleep cycle: what used to be a well-defined daily schedule has merged into a singular whole, broken only by sleep, an intermittently afforded luxury. Be it 4 in the morning or 11 at night, I can usually be found at my temporary office (the basement of my house) attending meetings or speaking to my team in India. The 'post-work hours' truly begin when India goes to sleep, and I generally spend that time with my family.

The lockdown, for me, has been yet another chance to find a way to build a new product, run a company, run operations a better way, find the time to balance the personal and the professional, and yet, somehow, emerge positively from the crisis. While I, like anyone else, was trying to "figure it out", I still had to fulfil my duties as the CEO of Epigamia.

For entrepreneurs like me, the goalposts may have shifted, but the goals remain the same: to pursue our dreams resolutely, and to have ownership of our future as we had of our past. The approach may differ from person to person or business to business, but the driving motivations are comparable. In doing so, I have had to maintain a delicate balance between keeping my company and the people associated with it afloat and comfortable, and not compromise our product, business strategies or relationships. My focus has been divided into two camps: a) the obvious one being, how to keep my company and people affiliated with it comfortable and b) exploring avenues through which our product can contribute meaningfully towards alleviating some of the suffering caused by the pandemic.

Epigamia is a contemporary take on the traditional dairy industry, and while our work relies on certain digital processes, other aspects are predominantly offline. Our distribution networks, for example, require on-ground engagement on a constant basis with collaborators such as local kirana or grocery stores, which supply our product to customers. In this way, Epigamia's business model is different from that of typical e-commerce vendors who cater exclusively to individuals and firms over the internet. Prior to Covid-19, a majority of our orders came from stores that were offline, and only about 5 per cent of the sales could be attributed to online transactions. With the onset of the lockdown period, many such offline stores had to shut shop, with only essential goods and services being allowed to operate.

As we commenced work under the lockdown restrictions, it soon became apparent that none of us would wake up to the same day-to-day job responsibilities, roles and processes. We would have to develop a work culture that further encouraged the cross-functional way of operating. The aim was to create a workforce that would be more versatile in order to mitigate uncertainties. We started slow, but it has been heartening to see the team step up to the challenge and share responsibilities with genuine earnestness. From arranging passes for the delivery boys to maintaining protective protocols with utmost precaution, the team divided the jobs that otherwise would have been delegated to human resources and compliance teams.

Suddenly, it began to feel like we were all in a (rocky) boat together, and if we rowed in sync, we might somehow actually be able to make it.

Correspondingly, some of our most loyal customers reached out to us directly, asking if we had any means of home-delivering Epigamia products. This led to discussions on building an online portal that could allow Direct-to-Consumer (D2C) transactions. We may not have been a digital business, but we did deliver to local kirana shops, making deliveries a less explored, but not an uncharted territory for us. Thus, if our customers were to order a minimum quantity (ten to fourteen cups) it would make home delivery a viable option. We tested the possibility by accepting limited orders via WhatsApp and email, and once we found the premise promising, we decided to go all in. Within a week, we introduced a simplistic but functional online order placement system through our website. What was implemented as a temporary fix has now become a key distribution channel and the overall digital business now accounts for up to 25 per cent of our overall sales. Such unexpected impetus in the middle of a pandemic has been a happy surprise and showcases the agency of an open and flexible mindset in times of crisis.

As we stabilised our online operations, the discussion moved on to how the company could contribute further towards critical humanitarian issues. We watched reports of migrant workers walking hundreds of miles to their homes, often on empty stomachs, and decided to do our bit by reaching out to those in need and offering our products (smoothies, yogurts and flavoured curd) at no cost. Members of the team even donated their salaries in order to ensure that we could continue to be a part of the relief measures. From being individualistic in our mindsets at the start, there was now a common desire to look beyond the four walls that we were trapped in. The pandemic was something much bigger than any of us.

Working from home has also been a learning experience. It has made me appreciate work as something you do and not somewhere you have to go. My team and I are gradually adjusting our schedules to better fit our lives, and we are enjoying it—giving people control over where and when work gets done, instead of demanding face time at the office. We, and the world at large, basically just did a calendar zero for the entire economy and sort of started from scratch. I also do not particularly subscribe to the term "work from home". Mainly because, the crisis has explicitly emphasised that in this digitally connected world, you don't need to work from the office. Therefore, I prefer calling it "working out of office" instead.

Although I consider the new work norm a welcome change, and I am a big proponent of it, I am also conscious of the opportunity costs of the same. The camaraderie between colleagues, and the social bonds that develop through our interactions at work may decline as connecting over video calls is a significantly more impersonal experience than meeting face to face. And of course, running into co-workers in the hallway is sure to spur serendipitous ideas, right? It is also a different experience for every individual, based on location and household dynamics. Work-from-home will be very different for someone living in the outskirts of Delhi as opposed to someone who is living in the heart of Mumbai or someone who is operating from Bareilly. One of our key team members, for example, lives with her family of ten, and is expected to be a mother, a wife, a daughter-in-law, and a prolific worker at the same time. It is complicated to tell her to work from home as it would disturb tenuously articulated routines. Needless to say, it may also impact her efficiency at the job. It is thus important to be considerate of individual sensitivities and apprehensions when implementing remote work directives.

All said and done, this shift was a long time coming and the pandemic has only sped up the process. It also shows glimpses of what our collective future may look like: working remotely from homes and cafes with weekly visitations to the central workplace for having essential discussions with co-workers in person. Perhaps co-working spaces will also come good on their theoretical promise and get to thrive. Meeting colleagues occasionally and sustaining personal bonds may also prove to be beneficial from a social perspective. If you ask me, we may have seen the end of the corporate office as we knew it.

On a more personal note, working remotely has allowed me to make up for a lot of lost time with my family. I can finally be more involved in my children's lives. I have two sons, a two-year old and a six-year-old. For the little one, this is all just one big party, where he enjoys every bit of the sudden barrage of attention he receives. My older one, of course, has a better understanding of the situation, being victim to the study-from-home set-up. Since his study material isn't too complex yet, I'm more concerned about the potential effects of schooling-at-home on his social development. The point of getting an education is not only to teach kids how to solve math problems or perfect their language skills, but also to develop cognitive, physical and interpersonal skills while interacting with peers and teachers in learning-based environments. In the future, perhaps, there might be more thought given to community-driven schooling systems or maybe technology will once again surprise us by making schooling from home more immersive, or maybe, we'll just have to wait and watch.

The Covid-19 catastrophe has come with hints of a silver lining. For instance, working from home has brought me a lot closer to my team in India. Be it celebrating our small wins and product launches over drinks on video call or conducting regular "town halls" to meet and greet, our efforts are channelled towards making sure that company morale did not suffer. During these weeks and months, I've come to think of them as my extended family, and that has helped me attain a greater degree of focus and motivation. Additionally, we found a way to expand our business's outreach—a temporary fix to the lockdown problem became a large contributor to our aggregate sales. Also, I managed to earn some brownie points for being a half-decent father and husband!

In retrospect, this crisis has forced us all to adapt and create, re-centre and re-align—and in my opinion, it has arrived as a much-needed good old-fashioned shake-up.

8

Delhi Police, Dil Ki Police

A Police Officer on Duty during the Nationwide Lockdown

Editors' Note

A policeman's job is fraught with a million challenges even in the best of times. In the face of a global pandemic—an enemy you cannot see, as the respondent in this essay calls it—and the "most stringent national lockdown in the world" it engendered physical and emotional stress that the force had seldom experienced before. What made it doubly hard for Delhi Police was that the force had barely recovered from the double whammy of the Citizenship Amendment Act (CAA) protests in 2019 and the riots in north-east Delhi in early 2020, when the pandemic struck. The Delhi Police's handling of both these crises had been subject to severe criticism.

The CAA provided citizenship to persecuted religious minorities including Hindus, Sikhs, Buddhists, Jains, Parsis and Christians, in neighbouring countries such as Afghanistan, Bangladesh and Pakistan who arrived in India before the end of December 2014. This act along with the announcement of the National Register of Citizens (NRC) sparked largescale protests as many believed that the law was prejudicial against the Muslim community. Shaheen

Bagh, the epicentre of these protests, saw women and children in huge numbers. As a result, there was massive deployment of police forces in the area to ensure that things remained peaceful. Another incident categorised under the CAA–NRC protests was the violence at the Jamia Millia Islamia University in New Delhi that broke out on 15 December 2019. Many claimed that the police entered the university premises forcefully to confront student protestors, which ended in a clash between the two parties. At the same time, another narrative floating around claimed that the police went in to identify goons who were causing an unrest within the university. The incident resulted in arrests, and over a hundred people getting injured and being rushed to hospitals.

The timing of the Delhi riots coincided with the visit of the then president of the United States, Donald Trump, to India. Police forces were deployed in large numbers to line the roads for the president. While the police claimed to have informed the ministry of home affairs about the shortage of policemen for dousing the violence (the ministry denied any such claims), the role of Delhi Police with regard to the riots has been questioned by various sources including Amnesty International that accused them of human rights abuses. A few reports called out the police for their inaction and their encouragement to the rioters.

There isn't a doubt that the lockdown brought a paradigm shift in police working. Policing also evolved as a human face of law-enforcing mechanisms under the leadership of Commissioner of Police, Delhi, S.N. Shrivastava. Delhi Police proactively took up the challenge and translated into action the saying of renowned saint Swami Vivekanand: "To serve humanity is service to God."

The police force was among the first responders of the Covid-19 epidemic. In the first year of battling this, Delhi Police lost thirty-four of its own workers while on duty. The total number of police personnel infected touched close to 7,500—not all of them recovered.

In late March 2020, the police headquarters also extended help to families who weren't able to sustain themselves due to lost sources of income. They initiated an organised food network among fifteen districts. These conditions also led to the beginning of community kitchens, which, as the name suggests, served food to nearby colonies twice a day. Police Families Welfare Societies also conducted food packet distribution programmes along with sanitisers, soaps and masks for the urban poor demographic. Under this, over 1.2 crore food packets were distributed. As many as 997 women who went into labour during the pandemic were also taken to hospitals in PCR vans. Nine births took place in the vans with the help of police personnel. Over the course of the initial months leading to the first unlocking, the government rolled out helplines and WhatsApp groups for infected cops and families to seek help. Personnel were given immunity-booster kits. Dedicated quarantine and isolation facilities were set up.

After taking over as the chief of Delhi Police, S.N. Shrivastava worked tirelessly to strengthen its presence on social media, especially Twitter. It underwent a colourful makeover, a change from its earlier formal-looking, dry account. The display image was changed to an image with the quote, "Delhi Police, Dil Ki Police". In a year, the police chief's efforts grew Delhi Police's following on Twitter to 5.33 lakh, leading to the growth in his personal following (2.33 lakhs) as well. Compared to the Mumbai Police (50,000 followers) and Bengaluru Police (13 lakh followers) this speaks volumes about the success of the campaign. His idea was: if someone tries to propagate a negative narrative about Delhi Police, it is our job, via the power of social media, to correct the same by providing proof of work. He leveraged this large following to execute the idea of "Dil Ki Police".

However, memories of the high-handedness of cops resurfaced when a shocking video of a police constable beating a man with the help of locals went viral. Despite repeated attempts, the district police chiefs kept on denying the video being of their jurisdiction. A sixty-second clip showed a man repeatedly being hit with a stick and baton. The victim was also slapped and kicked around. Though the constable responsible was suspended, the image of the force took a beating.

Maharashtra's population was arguably the worst hit by the global pandemic. Police personnel were deployed for many tasks including monitoring of home or institutional quarantine, closing containment zones and district boundaries, as well as contact tracing. In later stages, they were also responsible for aiding stranded workers in their journey back home. This, of course, meant that the virus would spread among the police force as fast as it spread among the public.

As cases grew, the way the police responded, evolved. Separate quarantine facilities were set up, hospitals were earmarked specifically for police personnel. Maharashtra Police Family Insurance Scheme also provided healthcare aid. Policemen aged between fifty and fifty-five were given low-risk police station tasks, and those over fifty-five years of age were asked to stay home. As Pune Police Commissioner K. Venkatesham said, "We had to unlearn a lot of old practices. We had to learn new procedures and set standards in place to keep infections at bay."

Mumbai Police also contributed to the battle against Covid-19 in a rather distinct manner. They reissued orders under Section 144 of the Criminal Procedure Code prohibiting people from disseminating "incorrect" or factually distorted information through messaging and social media platforms such as WhatsApp, Twitter and TikTok. The order also prohibited the spread of inflammatory statements that were discriminatory against a particular community and any information which could cause panic or confusion among the public.

The sudden increase in the roles and responsibilities of police officers hinted at the larger physical shortage of manpower. With officials testing positive for the virus or many showing symptoms of the disease, the number of police officials who could continue working, saw a decline. In Bengaluru, 940 police officials tested positive in the first couple of months. As a result, the Bengaluru Police Commissioner Bhaskar Rao requested officials over the age of fifty-five to remain home. To balance out the numbers and continue the fight against the deadly virus, Bengaluru saw more than 16,000 volunteers sign up as civil police wardens. The role of these wardens was to work in sync with the Bengaluru Police to help manage the city during the lockdown. They were responsible for checking identity cards of the people at check posts, accompanying police officials during night patrolling, answering questions, assisting in documentation and computer work at the police station level and enforcing physical distancing and wearing of face masks among the public. Despite the fact that this work came with no monetary compensation and added risk of catching the virus, watching civilians in such huge numbers come out to help was overwhelming for the entire police fraternity in Karnataka.

Dealing with the pandemic had emotional implications as well. Experts across the world have stressed upon the fact that policing during the pandemic is "emotionally taxing" on police officers on duty and this effect will be almost similar to the 9/11 trauma for law enforcement officers. To help with the job-related stress and emotional trauma that comes with being in a quarantine facility, the police came up with an idea: a collaborative video documenting responses to "what they would have done if they were at home for twenty-one days?" This not only helped boost police morale but also got a lot of social media recognition.

*

I am a policeman. The nature of this job is such that it is assumed that we would be omnipresent—expected to be available everywhere, at all times. I am often asked, "Why did you decide to join the force?" The idealistic response is the contribution of the job to societal welfare. While that is certainly part of the reason, I also do it because it's where I have experienced catalytic growth. Every day is different. It is invigorating and adventurous. The uncertainty of it strengthens my resilience and allows me to be more adaptable. Having the people of your nation count on you, respect you and look up to you has transformative effects. There's something to be gained from each day, from each department you work in, from every person you meet. However, this profession certainly comes with its own share of criticisms.

I work in the national capital, New Delhi, a sprawling city with over 20 million people. The year before Covid-19 itself was tumultuous for the city as it was witness to some of the major protests of 2019. The defining one being the controversial CAA protests.

As 2019 came to a close, I thought that the worst was over, only until the Delhi riots hit. From 23 February 2020 till 29 February 2020, Delhi burned. Hindus, Muslims, police officials, residents, women, children—everyone was brutally attacked during the communal riots that broke out in north-east Delhi. The riots resulted in the death of fifty-three people. We (the Delhi Police), Rapid Action Force, CRPF and SSB forces were asked to move into the area in high numbers to help identify injured victims and bring them to the nearest hospital. During the riots, we lost a head constable and an intelligence bureau official.

The series of events made one thing very apparent: the relationship between the forces and its citizens in the national capital was undergoing re-evaluation. There was a sense of mistrust and hesitation that accompanied these events, resulting in an overall crisis within the mindset of the police officials. The stain in the organisation's reputation reflected on each one of us at an individual level. After all, we all wear the same uniform.

In the process of tackling protests, riots and other crimes around the city, we were faced with something we had never seen before—Covid-19. We had not been taught to fight a faceless enemy. Now, we weren't fighting a human or a natural disaster, we were fighting a global pandemic.

The capital city had many challenges. We were manning hundreds of checkpoints and running numerous patrols across the city during the lockdown. When someone got sick, we would get a distress call and were the first ones to respond. A helpline was put in place that permitted procurement of essential services, commodities and provided transport to a clinic or hospital for any medical emergencies. The helpline number was flashed on visual media, and we received calls from all across the country. Majority of these were related to shortage/requirement of food and medicines, difficulties in travelling to one's place of work (from people who worked in essential services) or immigrants who were stuck in Delhi.

This kind of duty was completely new to us. We were coordinating medical transport, preparing and serving meals to people during lockdown, sewing and distributing masks, and whatever else was deemed necessary to respond in a city in the throes of a major crisis. By innovating on the job, and overcoming adversities, Delhi Police stepped up and took immediate, effective action. On priority, the entire police force was instructed to ensure there was no panic among the masses. It was also our duty to ensure that residents had regular and unhindered supply of food, medicines and other essential amenities. Besides providing food for underprivileged communities, ensuring supply of essential commodities, managing emergency movement for medical purposes, addressing specific needs (for example, senior citizens) and taking care of stray animals were also some immediate concerns we had to take care of.

Once the Covid-19 outbreak took over the nation, the popular anti-police sentiment saw a shift. From being maligned as heartless monsters, despite breaking our backs trying to do our job, to saviours of the nation.

A national campaign was launched with the goal to reach out to as many people as possible and make them aware of the efforts being undertaken by the force. We took to social media to spread awareness on Covid-19 and motivate our personnel. It was pivotal to do this since this was one of the largest humanitarian relief operations undertaken by the force. The streets of Delhi were flooded with signs that read, "Delhi Police, Dil Ki Police". It was a widespread campaign, implemented through billboards on highways and posts and stories on social media, put into effect to rehabilitate one of the strongest police forces in the country.

The message was simple: We perform these functions from our heart, because these are humanitarian functions. However, the use of social media was constantly being debated upon. While its widespread usage proved to be advantageous by sparking conversations about the gravity of the disease, it was also being deployed as a carrier of what is colloquially called "fake news". There arose a need to monitor activity across social media platforms. The only thing as important as preventing the spread of the virus was to fend off any panic around it. It was, as it remains, extremely excruciating to watch the masses ignore the rules around the lockdown. Being law enforcers comes with the burden of being feared by the public in general. The most important duty is that of humanity. Delhi Police isn't the enemy; the virus is. And we are here to help.

The campaign was launched in late April and received over 4 lakh follower engagements within a few hours. It was heartening to see many fellow policemen changing their names and profile pictures on social media handles to "Dil Ki Police". It elicited praise from the common man and celebrities alike.

Indeed, all we were really doing was responding to a staggering need. The Covid-19 crisis exposed India's shocking poverty. We saw hungry people everywhere, lining up for food in the sweltering heat. The lockdown left many Indians jobless. In light of all of this, the new campaign seemed to be working. It gives me immense joy to hear more and more children wanting to be a part of the police force when they grow up. The police are often, and unfairly, defamed as blind servants of the government—that we do exactly what we are told and nothing beyond. When Delhi Police was condemned for their lack of action during the outbreak of communal violence in early 2020, on-ground officers lost their morale. This campaign was a way to help boost their morale at a time when their services were most urgently required. You can't fight a pandemic with lost hope.

I remember the moment as clear as day. The Indian government announced that all individuals within its borders should remain at home for twenty-one days. It was terrifying at first. The University of Oxford's Covid-19 Government Response Tracker reported that India's response was among the most stringent in the world. It affected 1.3 billion people. The lockdown measures, which were later extended, were highly restrictive, allowing for only essential movements of individuals outside their homes. Its impact was immediately visible, and most prominently so in the large-scale movement of migrant labourers from cities, where work had come to a grinding halt, towards the safety of their rural homes. Official assurances that essentials wouldn't run out did not quell people's fears that the more the virus spread, the worse the situation would become—gutting food and all other critical supplies.

"*Bheed ikattha na karein. Kuch metre ki doori par chalein. Bachchon ko saath na laayein. Yaad rakhein, Corona ko harana hai* (Do not congregate. Maintain distance of a few metres. Do not bring children along. Remember, we have to defeat corona)." These words became a chant for me and other police officers around me. The moment Prime Minister Modi announced a nationwide lockdown, I knew that my duties were going to be reimagined. It wasn't far-fetched to assume that the entire force would play a crucial role in violence prevention, protection of child rights, education of the masses and ensuring airtight implementation of the nationwide lockdown. Since we were the most accessible and available points of contact for people, the nature of distress calls diversified. There were no more complaints solely about Covid-19. We were receiving calls about domestic violence, complaints about parties and loud music in apartments that were violating the rules and even calls seeking help in buying essential groceries for households with elders above sixty years of age. By the second month of lockdown, domestic abuse complaints doubled.

The sense of frustration was ominous. I could anticipate anger and irritation in most people I interacted with on a daily basis. As part of our job, we were continuously asked to ensure that social distancing norms were being followed, masks were being worn properly, etc. While some cooperated, many rebelled. With the larger fear of losing jobs, not being able to return home or not getting the next meal, the need to maintain social distancing or wear a mask seemed trivial. This resulted in frequent outbursts and arguments between the police and the citizens.

I've witnessed eye-opening conversations between my fellow police officers and citizens. "So you are coming to meet your daughter? What is more important: socialising or keeping safe? Go back to your home. This is no time for *milna-julna*," a constable said to a woman outside a colony in South Delhi.

The day-to-day work multiplied and diversified for the entire force. Crowd management was the most difficult and time-taking task of all, especially in huge containment zones. Personally, I find patrolling and crowd control in Covid-19-affected areas more dangerous than fighting criminals; for the latter, we can at least see the enemy. Even enforcement of prohibitory orders became a challenge a week into the lockdown. Shops would open slyly to cater to the ever-increasing demand and controlling them posed a constant problem. The overall morale of our station and staff members was depleting by the day.

We were guarding containment zones, enforcing the lockdown, ensuring implementation of home quarantines in over 20,000 houses, handling thousands of migrants who wandered the streets in attempts to go home. We also carried out high-risk evacuations in areas colloquially called "coronavirus clusters". Most of us at the station needed to be sensitised about precautionary measures to be taken and had to be provided safety equipment. We were constantly on the ground. By April, we had distributed 145 tonnes of dry ration to families in need. The situation was not all that different in other states.

In Delhi, we had to conduct door-to-door surveys in the city's containment zones, which became another leg of work and also required us to quickly digitalise. Hundreds of teams were formed to carry out a survey.

We were armed with a mobile application, SS Corona, which sent real-time details to a dedicated web portal set up by the government. Apart from basic details such as name, age, address and contact number, we were feeding the mobile application with information such as every individual's travel history; whether or not they were using the Centre's Aarogya Setu app; and if they have symptoms of influenza. The government had launched a mammoth exercise to screen the national capital's population for coronavirus.

These door-to-door surveys were first done in containment zones, as ordered by the ministry of home affairs. This was quickly extended to all coronavirus containment zones of Delhi.

At the end of the day, after sixteen to seventeen hours of duty, all I wanted to do was return to the comfort of my home for a bit of rest. But the stress followed me home. I was always afraid that I could have been infected. The trail of the communication of the disease was an issue: if one cop got infected, the entire police station had to be sealed and the entire staff had to be quarantined. To mitigate this potential problem, senior officials worked on devising plans to ensure that the staff worked in isolated batches. Officers who returned after fulfilling duties in prone areas and outsiders visiting the station were required to pass through a sanitiser tunnel, which uses 5 per cent of sodium hypochlorite solution, before entering the building—to reduce the risk of the virus entering the premises.

On 16 April 2020, Amit Kumar, a thirty-one-year-old constable, succumbed to the virus. He became the first casualty among the police in the capital. His demise cast a shadow on the frontline warriors in uniform. Following that, we heard of another death—of a young constable at Bharat Nagar, a neighbourhood in Delhi. My dedication to the job has never faltered, but every time a fellow police officer tested positive and was at the brink of death, it became difficult to carry on with hope and optimism. To combat the pervasive gloom, we constantly worked towards finding new ways to bond and reaffirm a feeling of collaboration—cleaning the premises together or playing a sport together. A silver lining in all of this was that the fall in crime rate reduced the demand on manpower, and the police top brass could finally give the stressed constabulary a much-needed break.

For all our overtime, extended responsibilities, unflinching loyalty, we received little to no recognition. We were and still are working to keep the public safe. But I can't help ask: Shouldn't the average citizen be more mindful of their ways? Couldn't going out for ice cream wait a few weeks? This blatant disregard is testimony to the fact that India could not have contained the situation without the implementation of this nationwide lockdown. Basic fundamentals needed to be put in order: the lack of dedicated hospitals, low testing capacities in labs, test results getting delayed, inadequate testing, etc.

Complacency and missteps (by both the citizens and the government) turned India from a seeming success story into one of the world's worst-hit places, as experts say. Public behaviour and administration's behaviour matter. While it is disheartening to see that citizens are going about life as usual, disregarding safety measures and not comprehending the gravity of the situation, it continues to be my and the force's duty to protect the nation in its darkest hours. It goes back to the reason for why I do what I do. It is to find solutions and tackle the uncertainties even if it is a little more taxing sometimes. It's all part of the adventure of being on duty. It's all part of showing up every day for your country.

9

Lockdown Life of a Traveller without a Home

Shivya Nath, Travel Writer and Bestselling Author

Editors' Note

The coronavirus upended the world of travel influencers. When your income depends on promoting travel, government mandates of staying home come at a cost. As flights, events and media trips were cancelled and hospitality marketers tightened their budgets over coronavirus fears, travel influencers scrambled to survive. Influencers, who alongside many in the gig economy, make money through freelance assignments, including promoting hotels, destinations, airlines and other travel brands, now faced cancellations of their sponsored trips. Many struggled to cope with how to move forward as the hospitality industry collapsed.

Those influencers currently on trips were faced with worries about how to get home, in some cases cutting their excursions short. In addition to cancelled trips, travel influencers were losing money as the public's interest in travel nose-dived. Number of viewers on their videos and vlogs, overall social media engagement on travel, and their affiliate income were some of the many things that took a

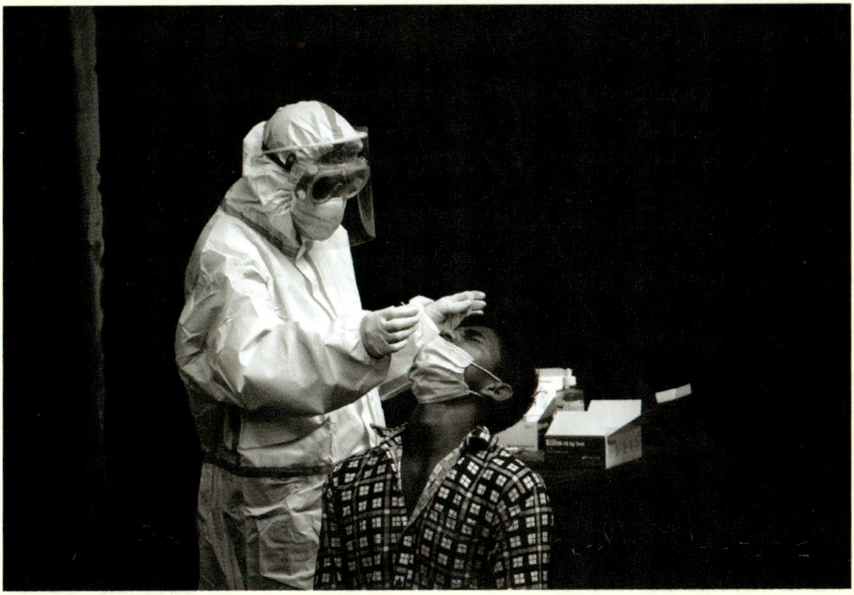

An antigen test for Covid-19, conducted by a health worker wearing a PPE suit at a testing centre.

Testing construction workers for Covid-19 on a site in New Delhi.

A Covid-19 victim's cremation ritual.

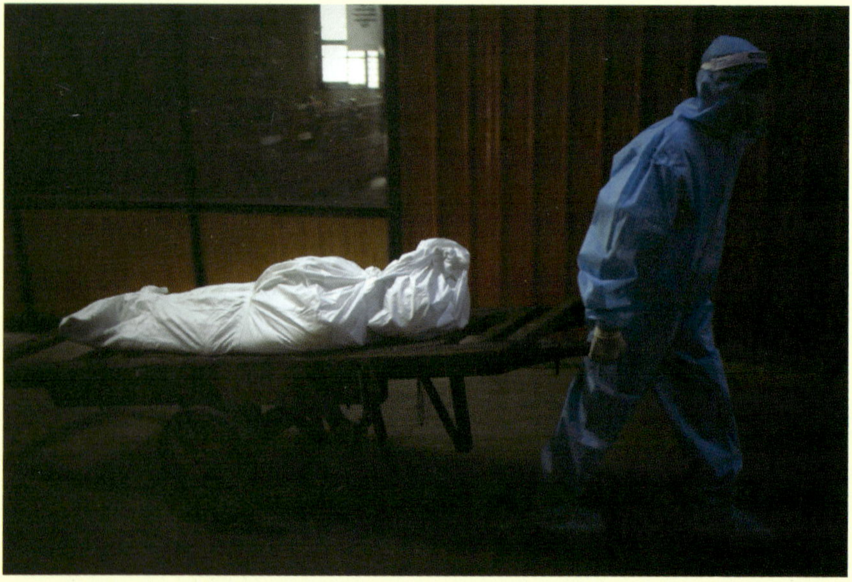

A frontline worker carrying a Covid-19 victim to the electric crematorium in Nigambodh Ghat in New Delhi.

An officer from the Delhi Police implementing social distancing protocols.

Labourers abiding by social distancing rules implemented by the government.

Family members read funeral prayers at Delhi's largest cemetery as part of the last rites.

Citizens resting at a Covid-19 quarantine facility as part of government-instructed fourteen-day isolation regulations.

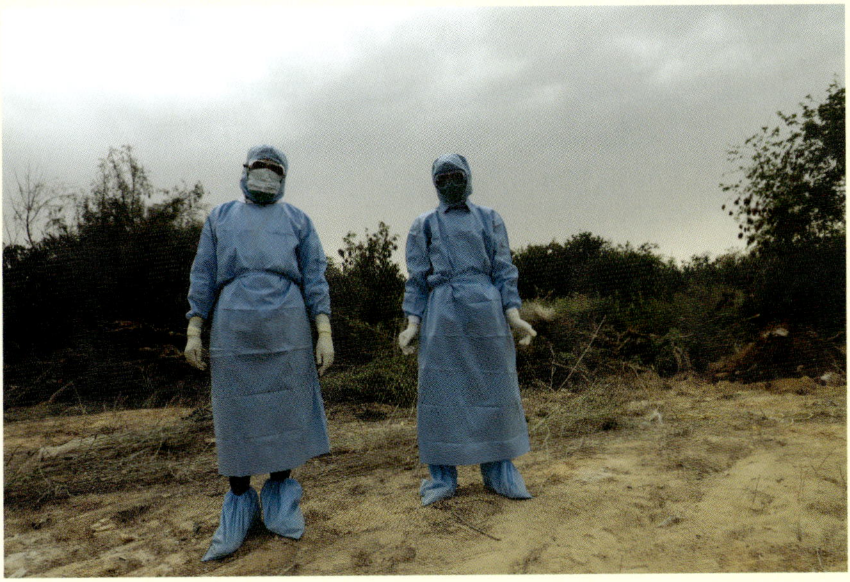

Frontline workers (gravediggers) taking complete precautions and wearing PPE kits to protect themselves from being infected by Covid-19.

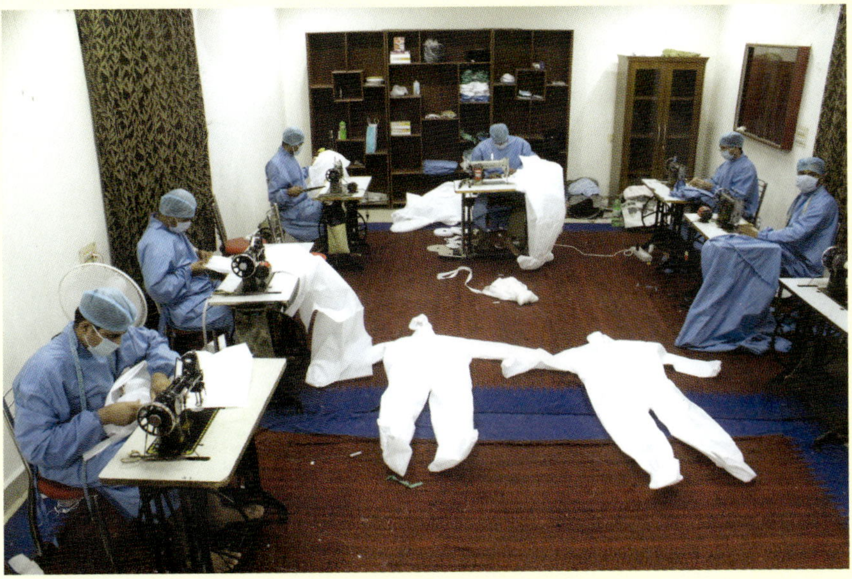

A manufacturing unit of personal protective equipment kits.

A typically bustling Delhi road, silenced in the wake of Covid-19.

Migrant workers and their families travelling back home after the initial lockdown.

A migrant worker with his child stranded on a New Delhi road, helpless with no means to return to his hometown.

Delhi's popular Connaught Place desolate during the first lockdown.

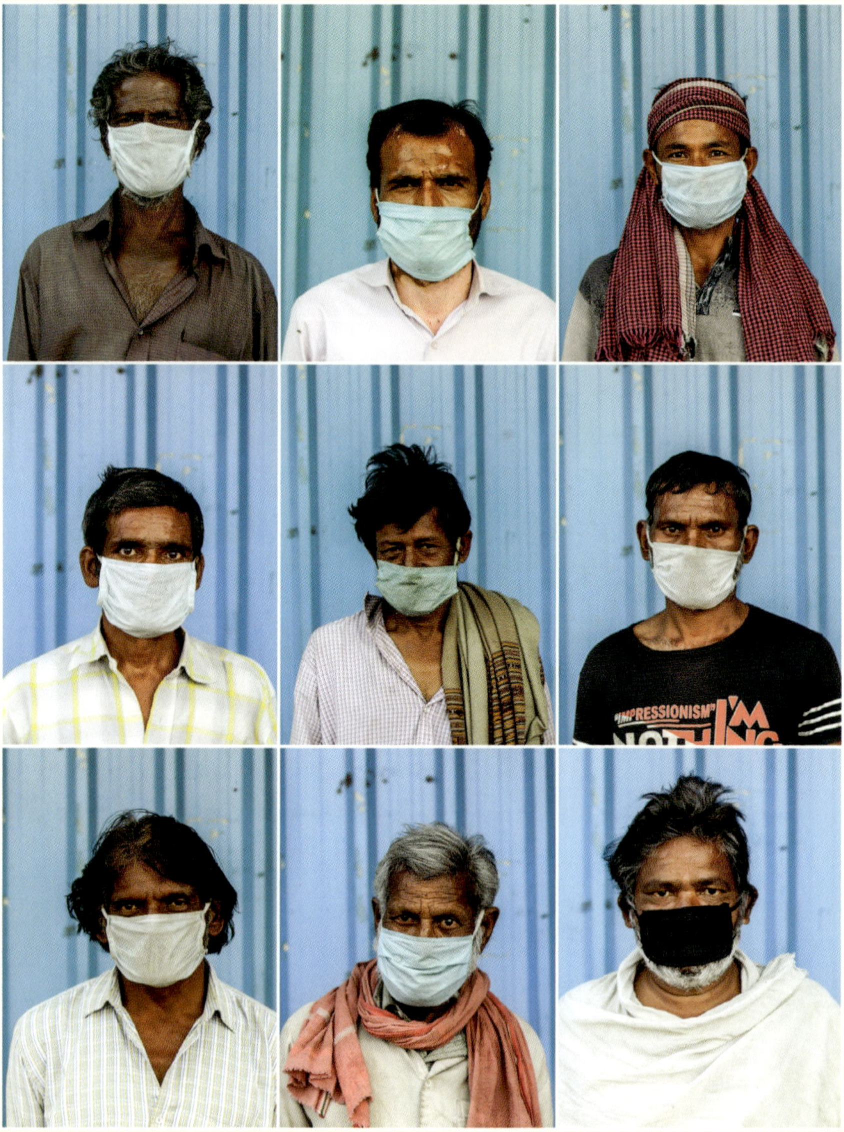

Portraits of migrant workers in shelter camps, waiting for a way to go home.

Photographs courtesy of
Md Meharban and Wasim Sarvar

hit. Hotels weren't being booked, people weren't buying travel gear, and the thrill of taking a trip was confined to walking from one's bedroom to the kitchen.

With so much up in the air, influencers struggled with what to tell their audiences. Some continued posting as if nothing was happening, only to receive backlash for being tone deaf. Others opted to pause posting until they could figure out how to appropriately address the pandemic with respect to travel. Some, like Shivya Nath, have nailed the messaging. In her blog, 'The Shooting Star', and on her Instagram handle (@shivya), Shivya talks about how she satisfied her wanderlust at home. She also talked about how to deal with the financial and emotional pressure of being stuck in one place and so much more. Read on to hear her two cents on being a traveller stuck in the world's longest lockdown.

*

It feels like yesterday when I was hiking up the moonscapes of Qeshm Island in Iran at sunset. Or falling off the map on a motorcycle adventure in the remote tribal Chin state of Myanmar. Or feeling awe-inspired by the electric "ghetto sessions" in Khayelitsha, one of South Africa's largest townships.

I've been called a storyteller, writer, photographer, digital nomad, Instagrammer, social entrepreneur, solo traveller and environmentalist. But in my heart, I'm just a girl who travels. It all started out as just a dream, a fascination for faraway places, a curiosity to know people different from me.

Back in 2011, I quit my nine-to-five corporate job in Singapore. I think my turning point was a two-month unpaid sabbatical from work, part of which I spent volunteer-travelling by myself in the cold mountain desert of Spiti. That was my first conscious solo trip, and the first time I hiked and hitchhiked by myself. I slept under millions of stars, swapped life stories with Buddhist monks and nuns who've spent years in solitude, and learnt how our travel choices impact local communities and the environment. It made me realise that there is so much more to life than chasing money and climbing the corporate ladder—and began seeking a different way of life.

Shortly after, in 2013, I gave up my rented apartment, sold most of my belongings, stored some in the boot of a friend's car and embraced a nomadic life. In the years since, I've felt at home in many places around the world but not put down roots anywhere. Having no possessions and no commitment to a single place felt liberating on many levels ... until I found myself in the lockdown.

Life began to change drastically. Mask-covered faces. Queues to wash hands in public toilets. Sanitiser sales skyrocketing. Accusatory looks towards anyone who dared to cough or sneeze. Eerily empty hotels, flights and streets following the travel lockdown. Places that were once plagued by over-tourism became deserted. The spread of the coronavirus, and the official declaration of Covid-19 being a pandemic, suddenly brought all usual life—and travel—to a halt.

Ever since this strange period began, people (friends, fellow travellers, readers) have curiously asked what it's been like to hang up my travel boots indefinitely. After nearly seven years on the road, living out of two bags, what's it like to chain myself to one place for the foreseeable future?

Back in March 2020, an unexpected turn of events forced me to abandon a multi-day trek from tribal Chhattisgarh to Madhya Pradesh. I ended up taking a flight to Dehradun to see my folks for a few days and figure out where I could slow-travel next—and hide out the brewing coronavirus fears. In those few days, my universe, like that of many others, overturned. India went into a stringent lockdown, state and international borders shut down indefinitely. Suddenly, I had nowhere to go.

The short visit to my parents turned into three months, and in retrospect, I'm grateful to have spent that quality time with my parents—something I haven't done since I moved out for college (at seventeen years of age!). In the past seven years on the road, I've sometimes wondered what it would be like to stay in one place again. To have a small backyard where I can grow my greens, to own more than what fits in two bags. Have constant access to a kitchen and experiment with vegan recipes. Build a consistent supply chain of organic, seasonal, zero-waste produce. And not have to decide every couple of months, "where next?"

After the initial shock of the lockdown, I realised that I had no choice now but to experience "the other side" of life. So, I threw myself right into it. Started growing my own herbs and microgreens. Experimented with vegan baking. Got connected with a group of local organic farmers. Tried to throw myself into writing, books and music. Binge-watched movies and shows. Surprisingly, I moved quickly through phases of denial, shock, anger and disappointment, into acceptance. As an introvert, a minimalist and someone who has been working from "home" for nearly a decade, the obvious challenges of lockdown living were easy for me.

Unfortunately, when the lockdown was announced though, my partner was stranded in a different part of the world. Perhaps because the geographical separation wasn't out of choice this time, it stung bad. When domestic travel gradually resumed, we went through a ton of passes and paperwork, Covid-19 tests and institutional quarantine, and took a leap of faith to move to a small Goan village for the near future. We now call an old trading shop-turned-studio "home", own a kayak and a small oven, and wake up to hornbill and peacock cries!

At first, it felt nice to have a schedule and all this time on my hand. But the days quickly started merging into one another. They felt familiar, comfortable and predictable. Waking up to the same horizon every day eventually became monotonous. I began to miss the rush of long land journeys, the magic of fleeting encounters on the road and the anonymity of being a new "me" in a new place.

Turns out, the reason I never found a place "perfect" enough to lay down roots was because I was never actually looking for one.

The travel industry has been deeply impacted by this crisis. Personally, my blog traffic dwindled, on-going projects were put on hold and potential assignments were postponed indefinitely. But my expenses were low, I had savings to bide me through that time, and I continued to collaborate with sustainability-focused brands.

At first, I sulked and worried that I've poured nearly a decade of my life into travel writing. But as I spoke to friends—guides, homestay hosts and others in rural India whom I've been lucky enough to cross paths with—my privilege began to sting.

As urban dwellers with easy access to the digital world, we can continue to work, study and scout new opportunities online. In parts of rural India, however, the lack of digital skills and tailored opportunities continue to be a challenge.

Sometime in May 2020, the scale and intensity of Covid-19 finally sunk in. It gradually became obvious that tourism was unlikely to recover in the foreseeable future and that despite the loss of livelihoods, rural communities were choosing to remain closed to the outside world.

This context sparked the idea of Voices of Rural India—an initiative I co-founded to help turn this unprecedented crisis into an opportunity to create alternative livelihoods by upgrading digital skills in rural India, while also preserving grassroots knowledge that is slowly disappearing. For perhaps the first time in India, we brought curated stories by rural storytellers to the digital medium, in written, audio, photography or video form, in regional languages with English translations.

In the short term, Voices of Rural India created a revenue stream for affected communities through digital journalism. In the long run, it aims to develop digital storytelling skills at the grassroots level, along with becoming a repository of local culture and knowledge, documented in local voices.

And for the rest of us, at a time of no travel, this was an opportunity to discover remote corners of India—across Himachal Pradesh, Uttarakhand, Ladakh, Meghalaya, Kerala, Maharashtra and Gujarat—without having to leave home! Even though I haven't travelled in the last nine months, I've virtually met a sixty-three-year-old woman from Kerala who walks several kilometres every day carrying books for those who have no easy access to them, an amchi (traditional medicine practitioner) from Spiti where people eat stones to cure diseases, and a young guide from Uttarakhand who visually documented the disappearing craft of likhai (ancient wood carvings) during the lockdown.

During the time, I knew that sometime in the distant future, we will travel again. Borders will reopen, businesses that survive will emerge stronger and we will get our passports stamped again. And when that happens, travel blogging/writing—especially the kind that's rooted in sustainability—will become more important than ever.

In the meantime, it seemed like those challenging times on the road—the border interrogation in Nicaragua, getting mugged in Costa Rica, getting stalked in Ethiopia, breaking my phone on the first day of my solo adventures in Ecuador—

unexpectedly prepared me to adapt, no matter what life throws along the way.

Some people say I was too young to quit my corporate job at twenty-three. If I stayed on a few more years, I could've amassed more wealth and experience. Some say this digital nomad lifestyle is unsustainable. I need to own a house; I need to own things. I've dismissed this unsolicited advice, long believing instead in the shared economy to find homes and rides around the world, choosing to accumulate real-life experiences over things.

In many ways, this unprecedented crisis challenged everything about my philosophy in the past seven years. But in the middle of a pandemic that shattered many plans, I felt really grateful about the choices I've made so far.

I'm glad I didn't put off my dream of slow travelling the world on my own terms. I'm grateful I didn't build a bucket list to tick off only once I retired.

In the coming years, in a world wrought by climate change, intensive animal agriculture, single-use plastic and irresponsible travel, we will face a whole new set of challenges. I'll continue to contribute to this planet in whatever ways I can, but … I can say with confidence, having tried it over the past many months, that living in one place is just not for me. I belong on the road, always moving, wild and free.

10

A Man with a Plan

Tanyel Kazim, Higher Education Outreach Practitioner

Editors' Note

In the aftermath of the Covid-19 pandemic, the world economy faced a tidal wave of long-term unemployment. Millions of people who lost their jobs early in the pandemic have remained out of work, and job losses are becoming increasingly permanent. The two problems—rising long-term unemployment and permanent job losses—are separate but intertwined, and together, they could foreshadow a period of prolonged economic damage and financial pain for individuals and families. During a crisis, the path between corporate denial and layoffs is often a short one. In the weeks leading up to the declaration of Covid-19 as a pandemic, brand owners and companies waved off concerns about the potential economic impact of the outbreak. Then, something changed. First, companies started restricting the entry of employees to their offices and encouraging remote work. Soon, we started hearing that most companies were considering layoffs to make it through the crisis—many corporate leaders were contemplating some sort of monumental financial action as a result of the pandemic.

In India, the loss of employment resulting from Covid-19 has been severe, far exceeding the impact of the 2007–09 financial crisis. According to the Centre for Monitoring Indian Economy, following the lockdown, the country's unemployment rates shot up from 8 per cent in March 2020 to 24 per cent in April 2020. Although these rates shrank briefly after the lockdown had been lifted, by December 2020, as many as 9 million people had lost their jobs. A Covid-19 livelihood's survey by the Azim Premji University showed that at least 20 per cent of those who had lost work during the lockdown were still unemployed and that urban areas were affected more than rural areas.

For Indians settled and working in other countries, things were no better. Many had lost their jobs and been forced to return to India. An Indian Express *report finds that in Kerala, more than 5 lakh people have returned from foreign countries due to job losses since 2020. Beyond numbers, the accounts of those who were laid off during the pandemic convey the sheer panic triggered by such a predicament. "Logically, I can understand it—the pandemic killed the travel industry and the company had to make some hard choices. But my son had just been born in January [2020] and my wife had quit her job because of complications during pregnancy. It was a terrible time to be unemployed," a thirty-three-year-old Gurugram resident told Scroll. in. He was still looking for a job as of February 2021.*

In a capitalist economy, the cost-cutting reflex is understandable from the perspective of leaders who have to ultimately make decisions that keep their companies afloat. This reality was exacerbated by the fact that certain sectors of the economy had been hit particularly hard by changes in consumer behaviour. In turn, this slowdown in parts of the economy and the increased uncertainty impacted the status of employment as well.

In total, approximately 114 million job losses were recorded across the globe in 2020. Employment losses were higher for women

(5 per cent) than for men, and for young workers (8.7 per cent) than for older workers. It was expected that economies everywhere will start to make a robust recovery in 2021, especially with the rolling out of vaccines. Yet, the global economy continues to face uncertainty and there is a marked risk that the recovery will be uneven. The latest projections indicate a persistent work deficit. According to the International Monetary Fund's economic forecasts from October 2020, the baseline scenario projects a continued loss of 90 million full-time equivalent jobs. While in the worst-case scenario, this could go up to 130 million job losses, but even in a best-case scenario, approximately 36 million jobs losses are still expected.

According to the International Labour Organisation, countries must make efforts to combine "the roll-out of vaccination, public health measures, and supporting measures for the economy and the labour market". Especially in light of the subsequent waves of the outbreak that many countries are witnessing, the focus must be on a human-centred recovery.

However, knowing these facts and managing the emotional impact of getting laid off are two very different things. When it happens, the mind cycles through irrational explanations: Is my layoff a run of bad luck? An occupational hazard? A natural effect of economic or industry volatility? A pattern that reflects on me and my abilities? Being terminated can be a devastating feeling, and often seen as personal, even if there is evidence to the contrary. This is where the power of perspective comes in. Hearing from others in the same boat and putting layoffs into context can help us survive these trying times. Seemingly minuscule actions, such as visualising your value by doing something you're passionate about, can stop the self-doubt spiral before it begins.

This is a story of someone who didn't let his layoff defeat him.

*

I am—if I were to borrow the terminology from books and media—the epitome of a "man with a plan". This has been an approach I have carefully crafted over time. I wake around 7 a.m. most days. Before rising and launching into the typical "morning routine"—chugging a glass of water, and checking on my houseplants—I write down three things in my bedside journal. Journalling hasn't always worked for me and I find that jotting down just three things provides my mind with clarity: something to focus on today, something to let go of, and a reason for which or a person for whom I am grateful. I have set a daily goal of 10,000 steps, a large part of which is accomplished within the house, before getting dressed for a proper walk around the block. During this hour-long stroll, I practise what I have come to understand as a walking meditation. This is time for me to reflect, or simply soak in the beauty that is London. I am fortunate enough to live along the Thames riverside and so, sometimes, I squeeze in a run along its path. I have developed a special appreciation for food during lockdown and have honed my culinary skills through a panache for homemade cooking; due in part to my multicultural background, with ancestry from both Cyprus (the Turkish side) and Mauritius. On my good days, I set aside time to play the guitar and before hitting my pillow at night, get some reading in. I am currently reading *Why We Sleep?* by Matthew Walker.

Rewinding back to before the pandemic struck, I moved out of my parents' house, nestled in the suburbs of London, into a single-bed apartment around twenty minutes away. Embracing my mid-twenties, this experience has been most formative.

Within six months, I learnt that I thrive in solitude. Never been someone to struggle too much with motivation, accountability or discipline, the quiet time allowed me to work on myself and develop an ability to plan and execute my days in a wholesome manner; days that involve waking up with the sun rising over the river, taking proactive self-care, going to work and … a few recreational activities thrown in the mix.

Suddenly, life strikes. A coronavirus outbreak and the first wave of lockdown hits London. This consistent cycle of habits, behaviours and routines I had worked so well to build into my day, began to quickly fade.

*

According to the Institute for Fiscal Studies, London lost the highest number of jobs of any UK region during the pandemic in 2020. The change in the number of employees on payrolls dropped by about 5.5 per cent from February to December, with around 649,000 people losing their jobs between March and June alone.

For Indians working in the UK, things took a turn for the worse across many sectors, some hit worse than others. In the service sector, for instance, over 3,000 Indian restaurants were forced to close, resulting in tens of thousands of job losses. According to Monder Ram, a professor at the Aston Business School, "Supermarkets are one of the most prolific sellers of curries, and large chains of pubs and restaurants are also entering this market, [and] these problems of competition and newcomers have been accentuated by Covid-19."

Further, according to ONS (Office for National Statistics), young people have been worst hit by the unemployment crisis: "The estimated number of people unemployed aged 16 to 24 years increased by 47,000 on the year, while other age groups remained steady."

*

As the Covid-19 pandemic spread, economies took a hit across the world. To comply with the lockdown laws, most organisations, including the one I worked at—a higher education charity—moved to a work-from-home setup. At my workplace, official meetings turned into biweekly catch-ups over video-conferencing platforms. Going out for drinks with the team on Fridays quickly morphed into virtual "pub quizzes". It was evident things had to, and were, changing—almost unrecognizably.

I've always loved living in the UK and have often benefited from its culture, community and opportunity. But with a surge in Covid-19 cases, I was disappointed with the slow, less proactive approach the country had taken to contain the pandemic. The UK's response to Covid-19 was noted worldwide for its litany of errors, such as delays in introducing a lockdown and imposing restrictions even when the benefits of early action was evident from the experience of other countries, and failure to ensure border control and sufficient quarantining arrangements. Moreover, the UK failed to provide adequate financial support for people so they could take time off work when they tested positive.

My immediate concerns upon hearing about the rapid spread of Covid-19 were the safety of myself and those around me. This was followed by the impact on my lifestyle and livelihood. These are unsteady times, but I saw it fit that the only way forward was to approach the situation with calmness and perspective. I applied logic to accept the reality of this misfortune. A pandemic has broken out, and it might be here to stay for the foreseeable future. Once I had made peace with this, I delved a little deeper. What can I expect to change in a country that was going to be locked down? A moratorium on usual activity; restricted social human contact; the cessation of public transport ... the realities started to unfold.

Back in June 2020, we watched epidemiologists and infectious-disease experts talk about precautions to protect oneself and others against the viral outbreak. Social distancing, working from home, quarantine ... preventive measures that were bound to culminate in a "loneliness epidemic". Experts observed that it would likely be a year or more before we could feel comfortable hugging a loved one or shaking hands with a colleague. I realised then that everyone, myself included, would find themselves locked down with others around them. This quickly became the most crucial paradox of the moment: with social distancing a necessity to preserve our physical health, our mental health was bound to suffer in the long run. This led me to realise that during that time, more than ever, it was important to not succumb to social and emotional isolation. It was easy to spiral into a state of desolate seclusion, pulled down by the combination of fear, anxiety and uncertainty—about our health, about our loved ones living away from us, about the future.

In the initial period, I found myself in a similar mental space. I missed the human interactions that had felt routine and insignificant before but were now starkly noticeable in their absence. Even for someone like me who was used to living alone, the collective void of suddenly being deprived of even the possibility of meeting someone and spending a few minutes with them was extremely challenging.

*

In fact, an ONS research report on mental health deterioration during the lockdown across ethnic groups in Britain found that Indians in Britain were disproportionately affected. Over 36 per cent Indians said that they were affected by persistent loss of sleep over worries related to the pandemic.

*

I knew I had to fight this spiral. Throughout my university years, my curiosity for culture led me to connect with people from all across the world. This habit had persisted through the years, and during the lockdown, I amped it up. I used to already proactively stay in touch with my friends and acquaintances, but during the pandemic, I increased the frequency, making efforts to connect with people almost every day, even if only through a short message exchange or voice notes on WhatsApp. A few minutes of checking in was a small yet effective way of keeping them updated whilst keeping me from drifting into a spiral of loneliness. Sometimes, we talked about our days; at other times, I would broadcast a video of me singing and playing the guitar.

I work in higher education, an industry that can be relatively slow-paced and rigid at times in the UK. Simple processes can become long-winded. This is why when the lockdown was first announced, we were made aware that we would have to find a way to adapt. Organisations limping through the crisis were increasingly likely to let their workers go. For better or for worse, my organisation's senior leadership had been extremely transparent from the outset. With a close eye on the goings-on across the education sector, they conceded that the economic impact meant uncertain times for our work activity. A month into the lockdown, conversations started to become more concerning. We found out that everyone's jobs were under review, regardless of seniority or position. A few more months later, I recall receiving an email from my manager along the lines of "can we catch up on a call?" Immediately after his email popped up, I quickly replied: "Sure, ready when you are." Over the next fifteen minutes, he explained to me all the reasons due to which they would have to let me go. A rather polite way of suddenly declaring me unemployed. The reasons were understandable—monetary constraints, a struggling industry, no respite in the foreseeable future, nothing I could argue with; certainly nothing personal. And yet, it was my job, my livelihood, my life on the line.

*

The higher education sector in the UK has suffered disproportionately in the aftermath of the Covid-19 crisis. Several universities in the UK, including the University of East London, Goldsmiths, Senate House, University of London, announced plans for staff job cuts to save money. Academics, already struggling in their roles due to the pandemic restrictions, called these layoffs "insensitive" and "despicable".

President of the UCU (University and College Union), Vicky Blake, said in an article for The Guardian, *"Staff are either at or beyond breaking point, but they are carrying on, supporting students and working hard. I can't think of a time when so many senior managers have so comprehensively failed both their staff and their students." Dr Jill Daniels, vice-chair of the university's UCU branch and an award-winning documentary film-maker was given notice in November 2020. "I've gone through all the gamut of emotions: anger, stress, sadness. Like the others, I'm over fifty, and we would be job-hunting in the middle of a pandemic."*

*

When the news of my termination sank in, worry about financial security set in almost immediately. I live by myself and am responsible for all of my essentials. When you live with family, certain areas of expenditure can be taken care of collectively, but this is not a luxury I had. With no steady income, relying only on savings, I wondered how long I would last. At the same time, I had another concern: How would I break the news without worrying my family? Luckily, on both accounts, my sister was able to help me out—financially, as well as informing the rest of the family as gently as possible, without setting off panic. The idea of looking for a job in a pandemic is daunting. But my friends, family and my girlfriend at the time helped me view the situation more objectively, even as recruiters got back to me with negative responses, citing the pandemic affecting businesses all over. Friends and family cheered me on as I looked for jobs round-the-clock, doing my best to not lose hope. My sister helped with mock interview prep, proofread my applications, made me a spreadsheet that helped her keep a close eye on the jobs I was applying to.

Since I was on contract employment and the contract was to expire shortly with or without the pandemic, I chose to look at the layoff as an expedited opportunity. I told myself that Covid-19 had just accelerated the process. While the prospect of no income made the situation far from ideal for someone like me, living alone and suddenly without any financial support, I gathered strength from all the support that I was receiving from my loved ones. I considered any and all jobs, industries I wouldn't normally look at ... and eventually, my luck did turn. The most important thing, perhaps, was keeping myself grounded until it did.

For me, applying some perspective goes a long way in dealing with adverse incidents. My situation, overwhelming as it was, could have been much worse. High-interaction businesses such as restaurants, theatres, casinos and cruises were struggling to reopen as the virus continued to spread, leaving many workers out of jobs. The greatest risk attached with being fired is that you can end up permanently detached from the labour market, and either you never get back in or it takes you years to do so. Long story short, my circumstances could have been significantly worse, and I felt lucky.

I applied a similar perspective in my daily life as well, which had gone from being something I had control over to a state of chaos. Suddenly, I lacked motivation and discipline. My "wheel of well-being"—eight slices of a pie I consciously choose to align my life around (personal growth; fun and recreation; mental and physical health; financial stability; romance; friends and family; physical environment; passion project or side hustle) became heavily imbalanced. I seemed unable to do anything but watch some of these segments suffer. But I reminded myself that the activities I chose to incorporate in my day—journalling, walking, cooking or the rest of it—are still mine to do and have helped me stay true to myself.

As I observe it, this pandemic has had three broad effects on people. Some were crushed by it, others damaged, with few escaping unscathed. Like many, I have taken a few hits—some harder than others—but when I put it all into perspective, I have nothing but gratitude. I take comfort in the fact that I'm not alone and that it could always be worse.

It was natural, dare I say, human, to have felt a little lost during that time and even now, perhaps. Lost in the doom and gloom we all experienced. How we were left anxious and low from the barrage of information hurtling towards us via media and social media. Such were the times! What we all tend to forget, however, and must make a conscious effort to remember, is that we are always in control of how we feel. Let me say it again: we are in control of how we feel. What we expose ourselves to is a choice. Every which way we respond to hardship, through our thoughts, actions and behaviours, is a choice. I firmly believe we are in complete control of what we let affect us, as much as we are in choosing what to do about it. World events have come along and passed throughout our planet's history. The bubonic plague, world wars ... we have survived before and will continue to do so. Of course, this is not to dismiss the crushing hardships and the personal challenges the pandemic has stricken us with and from which we have all suffered. In times of adversity, this is merely a gentle reminder to ourselves—to those with a certain level of privilege at least—to apply perspective. Or, to quote William Shakespeare, "Nothing is either good or bad, only thinking makes it so."

11

Don't Squander Your Privilege

Mudita Jagota, Patient of Spinal Muscular Atrophy

Editors' Note

The Covid-19 pandemic has brought to the fore an insidious flaw in society—that routinely, some lives are deemed more "disposable" than others. The way much of the world's reaction to this crisis has been mired in ableism and ageism is a pestilence of its own.

Being made to feel dispensable is not new to people with special needs; it is knitted into their bones and sinews. A few countries, like Italy, have reinforced this bias, actively deciding to deprioritise the lives of chronically ill or disabled people and elders with Covid-19. The rationale is twofold: they are less likely to survive, and caring for them may take more resources. This triage decision is not unusual during wartime or pandemics.

However, it is not as though public health experts have not laid out at least one way to help save their lives: If you possibly can, stay home and stay away from people. This image of saving lives is alien to many of us; we are used to heroes rushing in. But disabled and chronically ill people already know that stillness can be a form of caring. They know that immune systems are fragile, and outdoors not always accessible. "Rest" can often be disability justice, and right now, it is one of our most powerful tools to keep one another alive. Yet, young, healthy, affluent people disregarded the crisis and continued taking advantage of cheap airline tickets and using their "time off" to go to restaurants that remained open. Taken together, the stark message to those with special needs and elders was that they are "acceptable losses".

In March 2020, the World Health Organisation issued a document highlighting how those with disabilities may be at a greater risk of contracting Covid-19. Yet, much of the advocacy on how to stay safe during the pandemic did not factor in those with disabilities and their specific needs. According to human rights expert Catalina Devandas, "Containment measures, such as physical distancing and self-isolation, may be impossible for those who rely on the support of others to eat, dress, and bathe … Many people with disabilities depend on services that have been suspended." This infrastructural oversight was further exacerbated by public apathy, with able-bodied people disregarding the higher risks their lack of covid safety precautions would pose to the elderly and others with compromised immunity.

Mudita Jagota, a patient of spinal muscular atrophy; the highest ranker in her Class 12 examinations under the differently abled category; a smart, humorous person and a compassionate friend, shares her experience of the Covid-19 pandemic in this backdrop. Like every differently abled person, Mudita is much beyond her disabilities, and she does an inspiring job of keeping herself reaffirmed of that.

*

Very early on in my life, before I'd even started walking, people around me noticed peculiar patterns in my limb movements.

They were incomplete, so to say. While other babies my age started to crawl, I could barely lift myself off my belly. When my parents helped me up to make me stand, I couldn't support my weight. With time, the irregularities started to become more prominent, and my concerned parents headed to the All India Institute of Medical Sciences (AIIMS) to get a doctor's opinion. Multiple tests and many anxious moments later, the doctors diagnosed the one-year-old me with Spinal Muscular Atrophy (SMA) Type-II—an explanation for why I didn't have the strength to bring a spoon to my mouth. SMA is an autosomal recessive disorder that causes muscle weakness and restricted limb movements; the name of the disorder makes this quite evident of course. It affects the part of the nervous system that controls voluntary muscle movement.

But what many people don't know is that having SMA also means having generally low immunity and a compromised respiratory system, a significantly dangerous combination. Let me put this in context: even though SMA's biggest visible manifestation is restricted movement, breathing problems are the leading cause of illness for those affected by the disorder. In fact, they are the most common cause of death for children with Type-I and Type-II SMA. We are affected by lung underdevelopment, difficulty swallowing, sleeping problems due to hypoventilation, and increased susceptibility to viral infections and pneumonia.

Why am I telling you all this?

Because on the 24 March 2020, when Prime Minister Narendra Modi first announced a nationwide lockdown, the fear that had overshadowed my life in the preceding months was confirmed—that my life was going to change in excruciating ways. This fear had started looming much before the lockdown was officially announced. At a time when there was only a single reported case of Covid-19 in the country, I had already started going to college with a mask and would wear it the entire day except during lunch or while talking. I was taking extreme precautions in public and was steaming and gargling at home.

One day, my throat felt scratchy—as though I had caught a cold. I was petrified. I had attended a kid's birthday party, and a part of me was convinced that I had picked up the virus. I couldn't sleep all night, all my energy fixated on a single thought. *Please, let it not be Covid-19.* At college, we were a group of six to seven friends; before, we would greet each other with a hug every morning we met and every evening when we said goodbye. We stopped doing that, sceptical even to shake hands without using a sanitiser first. With my condition, there was no risk too small. While the fear of Covid-19 has spared no one, it has presented a gloom more ominous than the others' for me. I've had to be increasingly more precautious, more alert and more aware because, you see, unlike most people my age who stand the best statistical chance of recovery, catching Covid-19 would almost certainly kill me.

Life before the Pandemic

Before Covid-19 changed the way the world works, I would wake up around 6 a.m., get ready for college, leave home around 7:30 p.m., take the metro to college, attend classes and spend time with friends. My schedule was relatively light, so I had a lot of time to do things outside of studying. We'd often go to other departments in Jamia Millia Islamia University and explore the vast campus; we'd go out for movies or to restaurants. Of course, pandemic or no pandemic, accessibility has been a consistent issue in my life, so my friends would look for wheelchair-accessible restaurants and cinema halls when making plans. At home, I'd work on assignments or study for tests, before turning in for the night. Life was fun and had a degree of normalcy that I can now barely recall.

In 2019, when I picked psychology as my undergraduate subject, it was because I had been intrigued by the sneak-peak that my school gave us into the area. That was what first sparked my interest in the field. And then the more I read, the more I wanted to focus on a psychology specialisation. I realised the tragic lack of focus on mental health in our country and the severe shortage of therapists in India. Mental health issues are rampant in India and surrounded by many stereotypes. Having an intimate understanding of how it feels to not have resources to deal with your condition or being discriminated against simply for being who you are, I could immediately empathise with those suffering from mental health conditions. During the mental health awareness week every year and through various symposiums, I had the opportunity to explore the subject further, outside the classroom setting. My interest in psychology gradually evolved from an individual interest to wanting to do something for the cause and the community (eventually, this would also lead me to social media activism). In addition to becoming a psychologist, I wanted to serve the disabled community—*my community*. I wanted to work for their welfare and advocate for their rights.

24 March 2020

"I'll see you Monday!" It was the end of the working week, and classes were over for the day. I'd just said goodbye to my group of friends at college. Suddenly, the news flashed, "India is going to be locked down for twenty-one days".

When you live with a disability that makes you feel physically incapable every second of every day, you constantly look for a way to escape that feeling. The one that's worked best for me by far is spending time with my friends and studying psychology. The announcement didn't bode well, but I reassured myself: "It is only twenty-one days."

SMA is a degenerative disease. This means that the kind of muscular strength I had two years ago, I no longer have today. A temporary solution to SMA is physiotherapy, which is crucial to keeping my muscles in action. Without it, I would retain disproportionate strength in the muscles I use for daily activities—arm muscles, for instance, which are always in use, while eating, drinking, working on the laptop, picking up things—and little to none in the less used/unused ones. This disorder leads to what we can call the "wastage" of muscles. Ever since I was first diagnosed, I have had physiotherapy sessions every alternate day. About twenty-four hours after the lockdown was announced, my physiotherapist was denied access to my colony. Had he somehow managed to enter, I doubt my family members or I would have felt entirely comfortable coming in physical contact with him.

As the lockdown progressed, life changed drastically. Even though my parents tried to help me with the more basic exercises, for the most part, I spent almost all day constraining myself to one chair or to the bed—attending online lectures and webinars, or giving interviews for internships. It took little time for these long hours of sitting and the abrupt disruption to my physiotherapy sessions to severely impact my bodily functions, in turn killing my productivity. Daily goals turned into weekly targets, and it kept getting harder for me to achieve milestones I had set for myself. My muscles started degenerating, and I could feel myself get weaker. Earlier, sitting at the dining table and eating was relatively easy; now, I need to keep a pillow under my arm to raise its height and make the eating process easy on myself.

The constant lack of exercise has made my body increasingly stiffer, so much so that I have become almost accustomed to a consistent, simmering pain in all my joints. At the end of this period of struggle, I finally started my physiotherapy sessions again, but in true Murphy's law style, my physiotherapists' family became infected with Covid-19 and the sessions stopped again. Yet, even in the brief window of physiotherapy I managed to avail, I felt my muscles getting stronger. It reiterated in my mind just how much this virus and the accompanying lockdowns had brought down my quality of life—a thought that brings with it a feeling of frustrating helplessness.

Despite what people might mistakenly imagine when they see me, I have always thought of myself as a rebellious survivor. Not to toot my own horn, but I've rarely ever let my disability come in the way of my ambition. I got very tired very quickly of being perceived as the damsel in distress, of people asking me if they could do anything for me, of being the "disabled kid" who needed to be helped. A few short years after I learned about my disease, I had accepted that I was going to have to figure life out for myself. I certainly wasn't going to sit around and let SMA stop me from doing the things I wanted to do. So, whenever I set my heart on something, I make a calculated decision and create a clear timeline, and I make sure I stick to it.

What I'm getting at is that before 2020, I hadn't really experienced *helplessness*, contrary to what the nature of my disorder might suggest. Covid-19 changed everything. There is, of course, the constant anxiety about catching an infection that for me would be life-threatening. But the lockdown made it worse; it made me restless, sad. The problem was not that it was happening, but that it came with no notice period and a sense of abject apathy on the part of most people. I looked around and those with great privilege, those with no disabilities, were handling the situation with unimaginable disregard for others.

With the advent of masks during the lockdown, "mask manufacturing" grew faster than any industry had ever grown. Within a span of two weeks, you could see thousands of people making masks of different colours, shapes, sizes, price points. Some manufactured on a smaller scale, out of their homegrown factories. Others, perhaps people with previous entrepreneurial experience, started the same business at a larger scale. Either way, masks were the one thing (after sanitisers, of course) that was made mandatory for everyone to wear. Despite the mandate, I would see people stepping out into crowded places like grocery stores without a mask. "It's not that big a deal…" some would say, as they walked mask-free on the streets, "…unless you're old or disabled."

Unless you're old or disabled.

As if there is an inherently lower premium on their lives—*my life.*

Once lockdown regulations started to relax and people began stepping out again, I could barely tell that a worldwide pandemic was still on the loose. Looking around, I saw people going out to restaurants, malls and other "entertainment-centric" public areas. My concern was not that they were going out, but that they were doing so without taking the necessary precautions, knowing the kind of risk in which it put people like me.

Since the lockdown was announced, I have not wheeled out of my house. Because, like I said, if I get infected, my chances of survival are bleak. Yet, my parents, on whom I am entirely dependent for basic life tasks, must still step out for necessary activities like grocery shopping, urgent work-related meetings and the like. It is highly likely that they will eventually encounter someone who carries the virus, or someone who may have come in contact with someone else who is a carrier. Even while staying in the constraints of my home, on my wheelchair, minding my own business, I am helplessly exposed to the virus.

But all it would take for my situation to be a lot more secure is *empathy*. The problem as I see it is that most people seem to have none of that, thriving on one sole motive: *to protect themselves*. Not enough people are mindful of the consequences of that harmless small dinner party they host, or innocently forgetting their masks at home, or forgetting to sanitise themselves. Their belief in their own immunity makes them act irresponsibly. This wanton disregard for other humans has made me feel more trapped than SMA ever has; it has robbed me of the sense of control that I have sustained all my life through every hardship.

Rising from the Ashes

Not long after the Covid-19 pandemic threw our daily lives off-kilter, I realised I was going to have to work hard on adjusting to the new normal, without compromising on my health. I started with the thing that bothered me the most—keeping my friends close.

Honestly, it shouldn't take a crisis for us to reach out to people we don't see enough. But the crisis did become the perfect opportunity to spread some kindness around. Since the lockdown had knocked me out of my routines and handed me—and everyone else who isn't a frontline worker—a lot of free time, I figured I'd turn the pandemic into an opportunity to be a better friend. I'd reach out to whoever came to mind, no matter how long it had been since we'd last spoken. I didn't have any goal except to pleasantly surprise the people I care about during a time when every day felt like a dreary repeat of the day before.

The pandemic seems to have made everyone an expert on video-conferencing apps like Zoom. But I often feel frustrated by the lack of direct eye contact, the low resolution, and the frequent technical glitches. So instead, I found myself using the telephone—a technology I had mostly abandoned over the last decade. I rediscovered how the phone can be a hassle-free way to reach out, putting the focus on voice and words, not your overgrown hair or the distracting mess in the background. The lockdown also eliminated the nuisance of playing *telephone tag*—almost all the people I called were home and available. Even if they were not, the call backs came faster than it ever did pre-lockdown. Very gradually, I started to look at the small silver linings amidst an otherwise gloomy situation.

In some areas of life, some people with disabilities are now finding increased access than they had before. Mine is a locomotive disability, which restricts me from being in physical spaces that are not designed with inclusive access in mind. The lockdown, which brought with it a shift to virtual platforms, allowed me to attend many workshops and webinars. I even found a paid, work-from-home opportunity for four months, which was both a great learning experience and a valuable addition to my resume. But this was an organisation whose physical office is not wheelchair friendly, with only staircases and a very small elevator. Before the pandemic, I would not have been able to avail this opportunity, because a "work-from-home" situation was not considered feasible. When the world finally returns to normal, while life will improve on many fronts, I worry that these small progresses we have made in increasing accessibility may be lost. Of course, I would like to think that this situation has driven home the point that people with disabilities can be great assets in the work environment, limited only by societal apathy and the lack of focus on inclusivity.

Over the course of seven months—fluctuating between anger and helplessness and happiness—I realized that I'm even more resilient than I previously thought. I decided to make sense of the situation and accept that it is here to stay. Over time, I started feeling more like myself, started finding joy in things that were otherwise insignificant to me. I rewarded myself with a good meal if I answered correctly in class or submitted a great assignment, spent time reading books and articles outside of my course material, and strengthened my relationship with my parents.

I also increased my focus on social media, being a digital creator on Instagram. During the lockdown, this line of work seems to be evolving even faster than mask-manufacturing. I create content on SMA, motivate people to have fun with life, and try to make them laugh from time to time. August is declared as SMA awareness month and hence, during that month, I posted information regarding my condition and broke down the nitty-gritties of it for those who might never have heard of SMA. I found using Instagram as a medium to communicate important information quite therapeutic. It was a good way to also use all the extra time I had at hand due to the lockdown productively.

From the genetic aspect to the physical manifestation of the disability, I explained the various types of SMAs and their details using simple language in my posts. Another issue I've always been passionate about is breaking the stereotype of viewing disabled people as "becharas" or helpless. People immediately view you from a sympathetic lens due to your disability. But the truth is that we're so much more than that. Triggered by this emotion, I also posted about self-acceptance and debunked some of the myths surrounding persons with disabilities. I wanted the perspective to shift because I'm not dependent on my wheelchair, I am independent because of it. Therefore, creating content for social media has proven to be a great way for me to escape from the mental shackles of feeling helpless or unproductive. When I'm posting on social media, I feel like a different person altogether. There's something magical about doing things from behind a screen and having people engage with you and your ideas, taking my mind off the physical location where I am stuck for the foreseeable future.

Towards a Kinder World

The pandemic has affected everyone, without exemption. But there seems to be a tragic lack of understanding on how it has affected different groups of people differently, disproportionately. Those with physical disabilities, like me, are far more vulnerable to the impact of the virus; those with mental-health issues struggle with social isolation much more than others. When the lockdown restrictions relaxed and cases started to go down, I had the nervous energy to go out exploring all of two times—to the restaurant of a close friend that is specifically made for the disabled. Sometimes, my friends would visit me at home. All these times, I was hyper-aware of everything I was doing, all the ways in which I had to take precautions to ensure that these few light moments did not lead to anything untoward. Yet, everywhere else, I could see people starting to slip back into a sort of complacence.

The onslaught of Covid-19 has brought back into sharp focus the ideas of collective effort and community compassion. A crisis like this is as good a time as any to remind ourselves that empathy for others is the only way to make the world safer for everyone. If you have the privilege of being relatively less vulnerable to the virus and the social changes, don't squander that privilege. Introspect. Something as simple as putting on a mask for you could be the difference between life and death for me.

12

A Certain Powerlessness

Devapriya Roy, Professor, Ashoka University

Editors' Note

Working from home is fun as long as you are the one making that choice. It's not fun when (a) it is against your will and (b) when it becomes the norm for months at a stretch. Take it from Devapriya Roy, a writer and a professor at one of India's pioneer liberal arts universities. A typical classroom in a liberal arts university can be described as an echo chamber of ideas, debates and discussions—made possible by in-person, effective communication. Although the challenges of virtual learning may not be apparent from afar, the essence of learning in this method is far from ideal.

Life took an unexpected turn for the students of Ashoka University (where Devapriya Roy teaches). While they bid farewell to their peers and professors in anticipation of returning within a week after spring break, a global pandemic was declared. All pending assignments, deadlines, practicals and presentations had to find an avenue outside of the classrooms as soon as possible. The orchestrated functioning of a large-scale academic institution with designated departments for administration, faculty, catering, residence, etc., was disrupted. Both students and teachers had to navigate through their fair share of issues to keep the ball rolling.

But no one was suffering alone as the coronavirus-induced isolation did not discriminate. With the Zoomification of everyday interactions and meetings, Devapriya Roy takes us through the intimate space created and shared virtually between professors and students alike. The aim of this narrative is to highlight the change in the contagious course of pessimism onto a hopeful future.

*

Since I returned to teaching in January 2021, trading the constant hum of writerly anxieties I lived with for the youthful effusions of my undergraduate charges, my days in isolation were surprisingly busy. Our campus was closed but everything had moved online. Four days out of seven, I used to be in a whirl: I read student essays, sent detailed emails, and prepared for class, which was at 11:50 a.m. on Tuesdays and Thursdays, got out of my pyjamas into teacherly clothes and sprayed perfume on my wrists as a joke. It makes my husband laugh. Afterwards, I speak to a few students who invariably linger on after the others have disconnected, their restlessness and anxieties and private sorrows reminding me of my own youth, quarantine or not.

Later, my colleagues and I have virtual meetings, sharing notes on how to navigate these uncharted waters of online teaching. We keep our cameras off. (During one such meeting, feeling very bohemian and domestic goddess-y, I had propped my laptop on the kitchen counter and prepped for lunch, chopping mushrooms and carrots, when I wasn't speaking into the mic.) There's quite a lot of laughter and camaraderie at these meetings too, before we all withdraw into the strange new quiet of our lives.

At home, I have colonised our guestroom, setting up a dedicated space for my classroom at one end, upon the long low dresser, with my files and books stacked upon the bed in small piles. All the people in our lives who have claims upon this room, upon this bed—our parents, our friends and relations—are all in isolation, far away from us.

Conversations with them are elliptical, mostly about what we are all eating and cooking. "Do you have enough dal and rice? Are you getting vegetables regularly?" My friend Esha called from Leeds: "The supermarkets are empty!" she said. My friend Amanthi called from Colombo: "I got lunch on the table at 4 today." My friend Aditi calls from Nizamuddin: "There's this place which delivers great vegetables and cheese. Do you need any?"

And through these conversations about food we communicate to each other the things we really want to say: *Are you okay? Please, please stay okay because there's no way I can reach you where you are.*

My students are all at home too, scattered across the country. Returning to their parental nests midway through the semester has made them more vulnerable somehow, as though they are strangers to themselves, their sharp college personas set aside for the moment. It is oddly endearing to me. In class hours, we find ourselves reduced to these flickering boxes on the screen, fading in and out, cameras turned off for better connectivity. On Tuesdays and Thursdays, when we meet, they give me all the news, what's happening where they are: Indore, Jhansi, Mumbai, Rajahmundry, Lucknow, Surat, Chennai. It's mostly gloomy. (The young have a far greater stomach for gloom, I have come to realize.)

On some days, there is an email from Nidup, the gentlest member of our class, who travelled back home to his native

Bhutan as the global crisis thickened. He was placed in compulsory quarantine there, boxed into a room in a school, away from his family. On the days the uncertain Internet makes an appearance in that schoolroom overlooking the mountains of Bhutan, Nidup writes a letter, and if there is a missive from him, I begin the proceedings by reading it out to his friends. It is as though we are all characters in a wartime novel. Then, eventually, once I have heard each of their voices at least once, we get down to the business of our writing class, the subject of which is—irony of ironies—the flâneur.

The truth about the lives of writers, of course, is that a large part of it, the actual writing of books, is spent in quarantine anyway. And so, for the writer I live with (my husband, Saurav Jha), who is finishing his magnum opus, very little has changed in this period of corona-induced isolation. He reads and writes and does his share of household chores—the proportion of which has increased substantially—and worries about the economy, the subject of said book, and those currently crushed under the burden of its inequities. In the afternoon, when he wanders out of the study to look for me—perhaps, class has gone on longer than usual or I am speaking to someone on the phone, pacing up and down the hall—and I see him appearing, bearing a distant look in his eyes, it feels as though this is every other day in our life.

And so, in writing class, I tell the kids about the writing of books: it's like a lockdown, guys. You have to get from one day to the next, and the uncertainty will be mind-numbing. There will be all these other things happening in the distance, but you will feel a certain powerlessness about it all. You will stay in and save yourself. You will finish the book.

They murmur politely at the other end.

In addition to class, where we last read Manto, on certain afternoons I have office hours with students. Sitting on the guest bed, I speak to them on the phone or on Google Hangouts, about their assignments. We have run into a predictable complication. With the lockdown, they have no access to the streets or marketplaces or crowds, the spaces where, from Baudelaire's time, the flâneur has thrived.

And so, in lieu of the actual thing, we read, we learn to go deeper—to rely on memory to recreate familiar worlds in prose—and we learn to improvise, turning the monumental disadvantage to an advantage. How about they ask their parents or grandparents, the people they are in lockdown with, about *their* flâneric tendencies? About the towns and cities where they grew up, of which they have specific memories? Why not bring in oral history?

They dismiss the idea at first with the millennial horror of letting their personal and collegial lives come together any more than it already has—*what, no!*—and then, slowly but surely, they circle back to it. And so, at the end, our classroom comes alive with the specificity of epiphany—a record store in old Delhi, a *paan wallah* in Gurgaon, a photo studio in pre-Partition Mymensingh, a stationery story in Sadar Bazaar where a sixteen-year-old begins to work at his father's shop. The past and the present come together; it is a portal to a parallel covid-free world.

13

It Takes Courage

Shilarna Vaze, Celebrity Chef,
Digital Content Creator, Mother

Editors' Note

The pandemic disrupted the functioning of the entire hospitality industry and brought to a pause the collective experience of eating out. No parties, no weddings, no potlucks. Everyone was forced indoors with having to make do with the bare minimum.

Visual art serves the eyes, music feeds the ears but food is an artform that caters to all senses. You see, you hear, you smell, you touch, you taste. While the art of cooking can be practised in an apartment, a street corner or a kitchen at a fine dining restaurant, it doesn't hold much value if you don't have someone to appreciate it.

While the lockdown initially struck as an inconvenience for most, it turned out to be an opportunity eventually. Cooking became an avenue explored by nearly everyone—those who rarely entered the kitchen, those looking for a new hobby and those wanting to further their skills. With the advent of the Covid-19 special Dalgona coffee, more recipes surfaced online for people to try at home. Hence, despite not having the option of going to a restaurant, people turned to the Internet to satiate their palates.

This is where chefs and influencers like Shilarna Vaze came to the rescue. With her business on a complete pause, the diversification of her interests and livelihood online turned out to be a boon. Through her growing social media presence, she could reach out to her audience and churn out new and easy recipes for people to try, frequently. In this narrative, Shilarna takes us through the challenges and the delights of being a mother and a wife, in addition to her insight into how she made the most of this crisis.

*

Food is the ultimate expression of art—a notion I understood very early on in life. The feeling of embracing a good meal is primal, essential and extremely gratifying, extending to the other side of the table as well. This becomes the reason behind peoples' satisfied smiles (and tummies) at the end of a delicious meal.

I know many people in the hospitality, events and tourism industry understand when I say that right now, we all are in the process of starting from scratch. All those (especially chefs) who are making Instagram videos and giving away their bag of tricks for free are probably really worried about their on-ground businesses—restaurants, cafes, catering service. It takes courage. It takes courage to recognise the bleakness of the situation and the consequent hardening of your heart, because you have to "keep it together".

Like most people, I had a difficult time getting accustomed to the prevalence of a virus as deadly as the one we are fighting against today. My last catering event was a Holi bash for Indian actress Priyanka Chopra and businessperson Isha Ambani.

The entire nation had started wearing masks in public and I would often ask: *Were these protocols necessary?* It was not until the prime minister of India announced that the country would be under lockdown for twenty-one days that I understood the gravity of the situation. Suddenly, reality hit: we literally could not step out of our houses. A feeling of disbelief engulfed me.

Then there were the bizarre conspiracy theories surrounding Covid-19, from claims that it was developed in a lab in China to rumours that big pharmaceutical companies had plotted the scare around the virus to sell their products. New information would constantly come our way, either via social media or through news channels. Initially, I sifted through it all to understand what really needed to be done and what information to trust.

The first sixty days were just a blur. We readjusted, figured what "working at home" meant, speculated about when the situation might get better, and tried to make the most of the time. These unprecedented times had me and others in the hospitality industry grappling in the dark, trying hard to expand and introduce new concepts to stay relevant. We experimented with formats such as DIY kits or classes for aspiring chefs, while also profoundly aware of the fact that these makeshift alternatives were not going to lead to monumental profits.

As a business owner who hasn't overexpanded (our business does not have any external partners or investors who can hold us accountable for our finances), we were able to manage our overheads. Chris, my husband and business partner, and I were primarily concerned about continuing the business and paying our employees. We couldn't help but be worried about their livelihood. Fifty per cent of the kitchen staff left to return home. I saw their struggle first-hand. It was a sorry sight for workers in the hospitality and food and beverage industry everywhere.

There were talks around how, without intervention, there may not be a hospitality industry left at all.

While I do not want to incite panic and hysteria, I think for restaurants and the hospitality industry, Covid-19 is going to cause a morbidly high business death rate. My fear is that only the big restaurant chains will survive, eradicating the eclectic mix of restaurants that make going out to eat in India a vibrant experience. Even in good times, if chefs can't make their numbers, they stand to lose everything. And these are not good times. For workers (kitchen staff), the situation is worse. Most of them have no insurance or savings to fall back on. It broke my heart to watch them go through this misery. Where and how were they going to get their next meal? How would they manage if they got sick? How were they going to pay their bills?

Cooking became one of the most common hobbies during the lockdown. White-tablecloth restaurants and dive bars were closed. How do you feed yourself and your family when restaurants are shuttered and store shelves emptying? Almost overnight, everyone in the world had to rethink one of the most elemental parts of their daily lives: food. It is painful but not impossible to forgo some pleasures, routines and duties for the greater good: playing a soccer game, going to a movie, visiting a sick friend. Unlike these activities, though, eating is not only a cultural ritual but also a necessity. People were scrambling to learn how to cook. Otherwise busy husbands, children, teenagers following fad diets, middle-aged people trying to get back in shape—everyone!

I was speaking to a friend about how Google searches for cooking videos had hit unprecedented highs, and the traffic on cooking websites was skyrocketing. I was not surprised. If I, a culinary professional who can make dinner out of a jar of mustard in a pinch, was thrown by the pandemic, what did it mean for the average person? It was on me and other chefs (also digital creators) to help out. I remember posting a simple recipe for poha (on my Instagram page), a staple Indian breakfast, and close to four lakh people watched it; hundreds of them tried out the recipe and shared pictures with me.

As a content creator, it can sometimes get exhausting to constantly come up with relevant content. Your mind drifts into a state of apathy. When I hit a creative block, I often turn to my viewers and followers for ideas. For instance, one of my Instagram posts asked: "What kind of food would you like me to do recipes for? What you can make at home instead of buying? Maharashtrian home food? Freezer staples? Pantry basics? Children's food? Do you like desserts? Healthy food? International cuisines? Desi snacks?"

If it weren't for the advent of digital platforms like Instagram and for my extremely supportive and engaged audience, our family would probably not have had any new income post the lockdown. While it can sometimes get tiring, being a content creator is a feeling that constantly gives. It is humbling to see that people genuinely do care, as long as there is enough thought behind what you are putting out.

But with great popularity comes great responsibility. The audience expected content to be churned out rapidly, anticipated seeing a fresh set of recipes posted every week ... and all for free! Of course, since most businesses suffered losses, marketing budgets took a huge hit. In fact, marketing budgets for influencers are a variable cost and were the first to be scrapped in every company's expenditure list. Thankfully, I was still collaborating with one or two (relatively) mega brands—just enough to let us lead a comfortable life every day.

I've always been the kind of person to ask a lot of questions, and amidst all this uncertainty, my curiosity has only increased.

Is there such a thing as a work-life balance? Can one modify one's lifestyle to better adapt to work, and vice versa? Is it possible to align all of one's beliefs, ethics and principles with one's line of work? How do we build a community, share unfiltered experiences, impart knowledge and information, advocate for artisans? How does one blur that line between work and play till it's all one unified tapestry. Creating this unimaginable reality seems like a morbid task and simply going to sleep with a secret dream where I've achieved this parallel reality seems like a much better option.

It is almost as if Covid-19 is a chronic destabilizing force in our lives and businesses, especially for families. We were in Bombay for the first four months when all this was happening and then from July we have been living in Goa which has been a totally different experience. I have lived between Goa and Mumbai since I was twenty-one years old. My first restaurant was here, I fell in love here, I was pregnant here, my baby's first swim in the sea was here as well as her first food. However, if you imagine Goa as living on the beach (very few apartments/houses are close to the beach) with bonfires and barbeques and commune-type raising of children in a "it takes a village" vibe, think again. Doing any kind of business here is also really tough. Take it from someone who keeps trying every five to ten years only to have it implode and send us scuttling back to Bombay where business is real and even corruption is professional. Long story short: here we are, with no fixed plans, no intent on arriving at any particular destination, just clutching at our little family and slowly beginning to heal from emotional and psychological wounds that have been created over the past few months.

Chris and I have been married for eight years (been together for twelve years) yet the pandemic made us discover new aspects of each other—both strengths and weaknesses. Understandably, no two human beings are programmed to deal with so much constant time together. The lockdown had us working together, cooking together, raising a child together—almost round the clock. Trapped in the house, we barely had any privacy or break from all this seriousness. Our conversations slowly became constrained to the topic of survival—of the business, of the safety of our child and our parents. How were we going to get the business back on its feet? How were we to maintain an environment of normalcy with a baby stuck indoors all day? Domestic conversations, an arguably dull topic to begin with, started to feel more burdensome than ever. The news and the exaggerated WhatsApp texts about the facts and figures of Covid-19 were not helping.

Zanu, my two-and-a-half-year-old daughter, has basically grown up on the beach. She may not miss it, but Chris and I miss it for her. We are constantly worried about how we are going to make up for this lost time. These initial years, while not as crucial for education, are pivotal in a child's social development. I see her feeling awkward when she now meets other children. In general, every child has had to relearn how to be in a crowd, how to socialize. The concept of sharing, for instance, has become alien in these times. How do you explain to a child so young that she needs to share a part of her pie with another child? It's not easy. But I take comfort in the fact that nobody—no young parents at least—really knows what they're doing. It's all just one big experiment.

Before the pandemic, it had taken us a long time to make her understand the concept of being away from us for a few hours in the day, getting her used to being by herself, without the constant need for supervision or attention. Unfortunately, these past months have undone that progress, since we are confined to our homes almost all day. What worries me even more is that she spends more time in front of a TV screen than she ever did before. The education system, too, has responded to the crisis in a rather baffling way. Schools seem to assume that mothers everywhere have all the time in the world to engage in every single class with their young kids. They are being given complex projects which often end up being completed by parents, though unacknowledged. I can only hope that we see a shift in this approach.

The worldwide pandemic, the economic meltdown, the dissolution of businesses and finances, and a countrywide lockdown for months that could extend endlessly … these are strange, trying times. But giving in to the gloom is not an option. Chris and I have begun to make a conscious effort to find some time to unwind. We play together.

Lockdown has been hard on my marriage. And now looking at the past few months as we have turned the corner from Irritation Central to being ourselves again, I realise that it was because we were being too damn serious. All our interactions had become about survival. Grim expressions discussing work (or lack of it), how to maintain normalcy with the baby stuck indoors 24/7, domestic issues (the most boring conversation in the world!), news (I haven't watched the news for ten years now, it's awesome, try it), scary forwards on WhatsApp groups. And then the fact that you have no privacy or break from all this seriousness. Yesterday on the beach, I was talking about "when will I ever be able to do a headstand" and Chris just lifted me up and then I chased him around the beach and all the kids started running after us and it felt so good to just be silly, spontaneous and playful! It feels so good to get out of the schedules and timetables and the deathly dull conversations. This is what I call the "life of young parents!"

It takes courage to accept a reality in which your dreams, your freedom are under fire; but you must do it because you have a collective responsibility towards society. And it takes even more courage to allow your heart to start feeling again, even as the air is filled with uncertainty—to let in laughter and kindness, and to give out love without judgement or expectation. We are all facing an existential crisis, struggling to keep up with the old games of *work–money–survival*, while also putting the interest of others first—kids, spouse, work … the whole game comes before you. I miss the feeling of potential that life had before, the thrill of exploration—beyond the mere survival. I miss being able to make decisions that I feel sure about—even though others don't always understand them—for my family, and more importantly, for me. In the midst of this crisis, I need more than ever to retain my sense of self – to heal, to be free … to simply be. Of course, I need money, and I need to think of the future, of the business, of the education of my child. But none of this at the cost of myself, my heart.

I've been asking a lot of questions during this introspective spell. The pandemic has been an incredible opportunity for me (and I hope everyone) to take a break from a linear thought process. Often in life, we think of our lives as one straight road—the next big project, how to grow bigger, how to get better. By giving us time to think about the quality of our existence, the pandemic has given us a gift like no other.

To keep hope alive in times like these … All it takes is a little courage.

14

Covid's Primal Historians

Greeshma Anoop, Lecturer and Medical Officer
Government Medical College, Ernakulam, Kerala

Editors' Note

The responses to the pandemic can be categorised into two groups—active and passive. The passive ones absorbed the unfortunate course of events and found a way to "deal with" what was happening. On the other hand, there were those who responded actively in the face of this calamity. Healthcare workers, especially doctors, fell in the latter category. They did not have the choice of practising social distancing or staying away from the possibility of getting infected. Instead, they had to save lives by putting theirs at risk.

Can we ever be entirely prepared to deal with a pandemic? India's population and the lack of sufficient medical infrastructure pose a huge threat to the fight against a novel virus. On the one hand, where the recommended doctor-to-patient ratio is 1:1000, India stands at 1:1700. From working days on end without any definitive cure for the infection to treating patients with no income, doctors had to face extreme challenges globally. In India, however, an added burden was that they also had to bear the brunt of people's ignorance, fear and panic, channelled via violence. Reports of several doctors being attacked physically and verbally surfaced in India during the lockdown. The violence was rooted in the anxiety and uncertainty that the pandemic brought along with it and the irony was that the very people committed to doing everything in their power to save lives were the ones being thrashed mercilessly.

In addition to being victims of violence, doctors also had to face discrimination due to getting exposed to the virus . Therefore, the mental trauma of functioning amidst such an environment only added to the gloom. From the immediate reaction of the healthcare sector to the response of the state and central government, to the plight of Covid-19 patients and their families, Greeshma Anoop has seen it all. She takes us through her journey of serving as a frontline worker during the pandemic and tells us the good, bad and ugly of it.

*

Doctors have specialities. Fighting the coronavirus wasn't one of them.

I've worked as a doctor for decades. I never expected to be serving on the frontlines of a pandemic. For weeks, my phone kept ringing without a break. My patients wanted to know: how can they get tested? How can they stockpile extra medication? Can I write to their employees to recommend they work from home? One of my patients asked me how long she should stay away from work to avoid possible exposure, and I had to respond honestly: "I really don't have an answer to that." I am used to relying on my medical expertise, but the coronavirus had suddenly put me in new territory, an experience shared by many fellow medical specialists who served as the primary physicians of patients with particular medical needs.

Doctors across fields who are trained to care for very specific medical problems were confronting a surge of patient questions and scrambling to keep up with rapid changes in case numbers and advisories from governments and health agencies. We were hearing a lot of anxieties from specialists who were unsure of what was the right thing to do for their patients. The best medical advice for the coronavirus outbreak comes across as contradictory: To stay safe, try to avoid the doctor's office.

Doctors cancelled regular appointments that weren't immediately necessary—on a normal Monday and Tuesday, we would see thirty patients. In the weeks leading up to coronavirus, the numbers dropped to five or ten. As fears of the virus spread in local communities, doctors across the country faced unanticipated stress. Clinics were being robbed of masks, sanitising wipes and hand soaps. We didn't know if in two weeks there would be a surge in cases and we would be pulled in to take care of patients. We didn't know if we would be called in to assist frontline care for the entire nation. We didn't know how we would provide answers to the million questions targeted at us. The system was starting to get overwhelmed and so were we.

I am sometimes the last person that a patient is able to see in their final hours. Goodbyes are often conveyed without seeing a person's face for one last time. While treating patients, doctors share an equal emotional burden of saving someone's wife, husband, son, grandfather or mother. From afar, we may just be doing our job, but psychologically, it is more than that. Memories of the way a patient looks at me, the emptiness in their gaze, albeit with a flicker of hope that maybe, somehow, they will survive, are hard to forget. For those affected by the virus (and their families), even expecting closure is a far-fetched hope.

I needed to be their friend, confidante and their doctor—all at the same time, especially as the fear among laypersons skyrocketed. People with even a slight cold were afraid that they were infected and were rushing to the hospital to get tested. Apart from treating them, our job extended into rationalising apprehensions. I, and a few of my colleagues, have seen patients with symptoms of Covid-19 and have advised them to get tested. In some cases, families have refused to do so and have taken the patient back home. We have had to call the police and inform them of the wrongdoing in order to ensure that the patient does come back to the hospital. That's not something you imagine doing in the entirety of your medical career. This was the new normal for us. We also had to try and limit our interactions with the patients—something that we have not been professionally trained to do. So many fundamental changes came our way, it was appalling.

During the pandemic, it felt like time had stopped—and we existed in only one unchanging block of time with no clear distinction between day or night, weekday or weekend, work or home life. Our work continued for eight to ten hours straight, sometimes extending to weeks on end.

Every time I heard the alarm ring, it was a constant battle between my mind (that knows it should wake up) and my body (that refuses). Once I was up and ready, I wore my uniform. In the Covid-19 world, it was not the typical white jacket with a stethoscope but a Personal Protective Equipment (PPE) instead. Those months for me passed trapped inside this complex ensemble, which resembled a spacesuit. Usually, I wore it for four to five hours but sometimes it extended up to eight hours. "What is it like inside it?" was a question I often got asked. Well, your vision is blurred because your breath fogs up the glasses, there is little oxygen, there is a constant urge to itch due to which rashes surface on the body, and you feel dehydrated. The most draining and challenging aspect was entering the Covid-19 ward each day. Many floors of various hospitals became dedicated Covid-19 wards. While people throughout the country were advised to not leave their homes, we were encouraged to not go back home and, instead, remain at the wards for days at a stretch.

*

Due to the shortage of space in hospitals to accommodate the increasing number of patients, school buildings, train coaches, stadiums, etc., were converted into Covid-19 wards. The beds in these facilities would be placed at least six feet apart with no extra furniture. The wards were often disinfected with sodium hypochlorite several times a day. Although the aim was to provide separate toilets for patients, in most cases, three to six patients shared a toilet. These facilities could not have air-conditioners as it would result in the stagnation of air which would create an ideal environment for the virus to thrive. The environment became all the more reason for nurses and doctors to struggle inside a PPE kit in extreme temperatures. Since relatives were not allowed to stay with the patients, doctors and nurses ended up doing a lot more work such as changing the diapers of elderly patients, emptying urine bags and providing them food.

*

I've been called a Covid-19 warrior, a frontline worker, a god, but at the end of the day, I am a doctor and I just do what my job demands. I came into this profession by virtue of my hard work, academic achievements and persuasion from my family members, but now that I am here, it is not a question of whether I prefer it or not. It is what I have to do. At the beginning of January 2020, we thought that this infection would be similar to the Nipah virus that had broken out previously. Our initial reactions were that it would be akin to influenza that would last for a couple of months but go away without causing much damage. But that is not what happened.

I've been a doctor for the past twelve years of my life and I have not seen anything quite as deadly as this. It's important to understand the make of the virus to know why it is causing havoc. Coronaviruses are essentially a group of RNA viruses, which are responsible for causing diseases in mammals and birds. The word "corona" means "crown" in Latin. If you see the visual representation of the virus, it is spherical in shape with crown-like spikes jutting out. These spikes are single stranded RNA—containing structural proteins. So, the "CO" in Covid-19 stands for corona, "VI" for virus and "D" for disease. The coronavirus is part of the same family of viruses such as SARS and MERS, but is a new variant.

Over the years, industrialisation has led to a significant overlap between human and animal habitats. Due to human encroachment and expansion into wildlife spaces, more humans are coming in contact with new species that contain dangerous diseases. Therefore, while Covid-19 primarily affects mammals and birds, due to the increased interaction between humans and animals, they cause respiratory tract infections in human beings that could range from mild to chronic. While Covid-19 may not cause as many deaths as the previous strains, what makes it extremely dangerous is the fact that it is highly contagious. The way to measure the contagiousness of a disease is by referring to its rate. Keeping this in mind, the rate of infection for Covid-19 is pegged at R-3, also known as "rate of 3". This means that for every one person that gets infected, they will potentially infect three more people. To put this rate in perspective, consider the rate of seasonal flu that stood at

R-1.4. The rate of infection for Covid-19 makes it twice as hard to contain.

I've lost count of the number of Covid-19 patients I treated. Unfortunately, not all of them survived. The hardest part about my job is announcing the death of a patient. The pride and joy of saving lives and receiving comments like, "You are God in disguise" are squashed in that moment. With such a highly infectious disease floating around with no cure, prevention was of utmost importance. Requesting people to wear masks, gloves, face shields, to avoid touching their eyes, nose and mouth with unwashed hands; to avoid close contact or going to crowded places; to stay at home if they are sick; to cover their mouth while coughing and sneezing or wearing a face mask, became part of my everyday speech. The feeling of helplessness was being experienced by all—patients, doctors, relatives, authorities, etc. Due to the sheer confusion and burden during the peak months, there were unfortunate instances and lapses that plagued hospitals. In a few cases, after the death of a Covid-19 patient, relatives weren't informed for two to three days. Dead bodies of patients sometimes ended up reaching the wrong families and, in some cases, patients were wrongly declared dead. Chaos is the word that truly sums up the situation on the ground.

Apart from the shortage of beds, there was another shortage being faced by healthcare workers in other states—PPE kits. In two of the largest states in India, Maharashtra and Uttar Pradesh, health officials faced severe shortage of protective equipment and blamed the supply from the manufacturers for the same. In states like Bihar, healthcare workers were only provided with masks and gloves but not the coveralls.

The initial days were extremely tough. I don't remember when I smiled in that period. I was mostly depressed without any connection with my family, my parents, or the outside world. I couldn't speak to them for the first couple of weeks that I was on duty. Everything from waking up to eating to sleeping to working was at the hospital. I began to smell hospital-like—the crisp, chemical scent became a constant companion. But eventually, the panic settled in. A few sick Covid-19 patients I managed in emergency refused intensive care when it became clear that their families would not be permitted to stay with them. In nursing homes as well, patients couldn't see their families for months. If video chats are soulless to us, how must it feel to say goodbye via text? A young fellow doctor's voice broke as she described her day to me, going from one sick or dying patient's room to another with her iPad, digitally connecting the patients to their relatives at home and witnessing over and over families falling apart with grief.

This is why, despite the risk, I still see my family. When the doctor in me advocated for isolation, my family told me firmly that if they were to die from Covid-19, they would rather catch it from me. Ever the Buddhist, they said, "We will all die, it just may be sooner because of the virus."

At the onset, with immediate lockdown rules being implemented, the strict regulations in place, India was applauded for its grip on the situation. It seemed as though the country had managed to shelter itself from the pandemic and the floodgates of widespread infections. However, it was soon highlighted that while India may be technically behind other countries in the number of cases, the statistics were hardly exhaustive. Cases in rural communities, and many states were not being reported. Healthcare access was limited and was not reaching most infected people across the country. Many states did not have a tiered healthcare infrastructure that could refer patients from local clinics to hospitals. "Existing vacancies haven't been fulfilled, even as government-run hospitals struggle without adequate manpower," said Inayat Singh Kakar, a public health researcher with the People's Health Movement in New Delhi. Most ventilators are available only in private hospitals, and even then, they're concentrated in just seven states. All of this serves to drive desperate patients towards private healthcare—if they can afford it. The mortality rates for those above sixty-five years of age were lower than those in middle age because older patients were likely to be wealthier and likely had access to better care.

Something I remain grateful for is the way Kerala managed to tackle the virus in the beginning. While the country was apprehensive about the burden the healthcare sector would have to face, our health minister K.K. Shailaja, also known as Shailaja Teacher, was a huge inspiration. She provided us with enough PPE kits, forty ICU beds, more than 600 beds and enough ventilators. Therefore, my hospital did not have to face any shortages in terms of equipment and technology. The "Kerala model" was termed a success. But this was just one hospital and unfortunately, an anomaly when compared to the state of hospitals overall in India. It is well known that our country's medical infrastructure is not robust enough to tackle a pandemic of this scale. Upon observing the contagiousness of the virus at the initial stages, we knew that we'd be staring at a shortage of ICU beds in hospitals very soon. The rate of increase in Covid-19 cases was nowhere near aligning with the number of beds available. A statistical analysis conducted by researchers in a mathematical institute in Chennai revealed that the number of Covid-19 patients in India who require ICU facilities may exceed the existing inventory of about 32,000 dedicated ICU beds by July-end. Their estimates pointed to 30,000–40,000 Covid-19 patients requiring ICUs in the country. However, when juxtaposed with the data provided by the Union Ministry of Health and Family Welfare, the reality was scary. The country only had 32,362 ICU beds dedicated for Covid-19 patients, excluding the 1,20,104 oxygen-supported and 8,91,828 isolation beds. September 2020 proved to be the worst month. The first wave of the coronavirus peaked during this period, recording an average of 97,000 cases each day and over a thousand deaths. Calling this period scary would be a gross understatement.

A lot of people ask me what exactly I did in the ICU or how it feels after treating patients who had Covid-19. To them, I say that our interaction was not only limited to a patient per se. We also had to take samples from a dead body in order to declare whether the patient was Covid-19 positive or negative. For that, we had to take nasal swabs from a dead body before we informed the family. If the patient was positive, the family was not allowed near the body. The protocols required it to be put inside a bag through which only the eyes of the person were visible. That entire process was both physically and mentally painful.

After working for a couple of days, doctors were required to quarantine for fourteen days before they could resume. I would get tested and if my result was negative, I'd go back to work. In my quarantine days, I taught at the medical school in Ernakulam to escape the monotony and too much thinking. After the initial months, when we finally settled into the uneasiness, I also went to meet my son, husband and parents regularly. Instead of complaining about the little time we got, we enjoyed and soaked in those moments as much as we could.

Amidst this gloom, it was disheartening to see that some people didn't understand what we were doing for them. If you go back to the initial stages of the lockdown, there were reports of locals attacking and also spitting at health workers in Kerala. Since the beginning of the outbreak, healthcare providers have been shown more support, solidarity and gratitude than they ever have. Yet, attacks on healthcare workers were continuously reported. It was jarring to see that while the nation came together to salute healthcare workers they were also being pelted with stones.

Ensuring access to health services is the cornerstone of a successful health response. Any verbal or physical act of violence, obstruction or threat that interferes with the availability, access and delivery of such services is defined as attack on healthcare by the World Health Organisation (WHO). The nature of attacks on healthcare related to Covid-19 varied greatly across contexts and ranged from the use of heavy weapons targeting health facilities to the stigmatisation of healthcare workers. Ultimately, whether they took the form of a cyberattack or a physical assault, they deprived people of urgently needed care, endangered healthcare providers, and undermined health systems. The Covid-19 pandemic put some health systems under immense pressure and stretched others beyond their capacity. As such, responding to this public health emergency and successfully minimising its impact required every health resource to be leveraged. Failure to protect healthcare workers in this rapidly changing context exposed health systems to critical gaps in services when they were most needed, and could have had a long-lasting impact on the health and well-being of populations. Tomorrow, if any of the perpetrators got infected and came to the hospital seeking treatment, there would be no room for vengeance or revenge. They will classify as our patients and we would need to treat them.

We were fighting not just the coronavirus, but also increasingly combating a never-ending scourge of misinformation about the disease that was hurting patients. We had to regularly treat people who were more inclined to believe what they read on WhatsApp forwards or Facebook than what a medical professional told them. We had grown accustomed to dealing with patients misled by online information, a phenomenon we call "Dr Google" or what journalist Ravish Kumar calls "WhatsApp University". But, in a situation as grave as this, we were finding it extremely difficult to fight these amplified fringe theories. There were conspiratorial whispers on social media that the coronavirus had been cooked up in a secret government lab in China. There were bogus medicines, gels, liquids, powders that claimed to immunise one against the virus. There were false claims about governments and celebrities. The illness was spiralling out of control. There was so much inaccurate information about the virus that WHO said it was confronting an "infodemic".

Having said that, there have also been a few instances that made it bearable. Some of my patients would come up to me and say, "Madam, can I get a glimpse of your face once without the PPE? I just want to see you and thank you." I would send them a picture of me over WhatsApp and after a couple of days, they would call me and thank me once again for treating them. Slowly, I began finding joy in these little things—the small gestures, the sincere emotions and the earnest intentions.

A sense of relief does ensue when you realise that the toughest part of this battle is indeed over. The main challenge lay in navigating all the panic and finally reaching a state where there was some kind of a structure in place. We made our way through the worst. Hence, I believed that the situation and its aspects—the severity of infection, the spread of cases, the mental toll, the restriction on movement—would slowly become better. Yet, I was affected the most when I was away from the madness, alone with my thoughts. A fear of uncertainty surrounded me while the constant stream of new information made it all the more tangible. Saving lives will always remain a part of a doctor's job—as a prerogative or as a duty to the nation. When put into perspective, the efforts, the sacrifices and the emotional turmoil suddenly tastes sweet, because our actions in those peak moments changed the course of history. Few were lucky to be bestowed with that level of responsibility.

The philosopher Kierkegaard said that life can only be understood backwards, but it must be lived forwards. The mistakes that seem so obvious now may be viewed as unavoidable slips. Each country may have its own set of mea culpas in dealing with a disease so relentless that humanity could never have controlled it. Some decisions, their menace invisible now, may prove hardest to bear. When lockdown restrictions eased, people breathed a sigh of relief and came up for air like spring bulbs. The feeling was that we had dodged a bullet. At the hospital though, we suspected Covid-19 would come back for us later. January, February, March 2021? It was just a matter of time. The unlock after the first wave had only bought us a reprieve: time to stockpile and prepare. But when the second wave hit, that time seemed like a precious gift. As the cases increased, the plans that we had refined over those months were implemented with meticulous precision. Of course, not every hospital fared the same.

In 2020, most states did not invest in the healthcare sector believing the Covid-19 crisis would be over in a year. However, Dr R. Venugopal, deputy chief controller of explosives, Petroleum and Explosives Safety (PESO), and now nodal officer (medical oxygen monitoring), Kerala, was worried as he anticipated the demand for oxygen cylinders to go up to over 100 MT per day, as the infection rate would shoot up in the densely populated state. When his suspicion became the reality in 2021, and India began "gasping for air", Kerala became a supplier of oxygen. It supplied to Tamil Nadu, Karnataka and to Lakshadweep. We were producing 199 MT a day of liquid oxygen with Inox Air Products, a private limited company in Palakkad, supplying 147 tonnes, the PSU Kerala Minerals and Metals Ltd seven tonnes, Bharat Petroleum Corporation Ltd 0.32 tonnes, Cochin Shipyard 5.4 tonnes and the 11 air separation units (ASU) producing the rest.

It was saddening, to say the least, to witness India's healthcare system crumbling under the strain. It broke my heart to see patients die as they waited for hospital beds or oxygen. Social media was flooded with requests for plasma donors and oxygen cylinders and as for the doctors, we were just fighting every day. Struggling, yet putting our lives at risk to save the lives of others. If there ever was a time to be selfless, that was it. The Indian Medical Association reported (as of 1 June 2021) that 594 doctors (most of them in Delhi) died in the Covid-19 second wave. Despite these frightening figures, we continued to wake up every day, put on our PPE kits and showed up to work in the Covid-19 wards. It was not easy to be a medical worker in a time that resembled an apocalypse, but it gave me pride, satisfaction and hope to be able to help my country and its citizens.

Were we scared that we would get the disease too? Yes, but at least we would have known that most of us will get better. Maybe it was the unknown that was so frightening back in 2020. Thankfully, the health system still had capacity after months of preparation, but if we had not tried to control the numbers as strictly as possible, the unnecessary deaths would have haunted us. Still, I wonder, if in trying to suppress it in such an inhuman manner, were we allowing this virus—which was the antithesis of humanity—to win anyway? A question I asked myself repeatedly was: Is Covid-19 scaring us away from our humanity? To me, the biggest threat of SARS-CoV-2 was not its virulence, it was the way it slowly eroded what it meant to be human. First it took away touch and that delicious proximity of a spontaneous hug. Then it took away social gatherings and shared meals. Now with mandatory masks we even lose the warming delight of a smile shared with a stranger. Crinkling eyes at them when they are about to pass just doesn't seem right.

In the hospital, this loss was even more glaring. I still remember the catharsis of hugging the nurse who helped me look after a patient who had deteriorated unexpectedly in May. Later, we stood apart, in silence, shielded from each other by layers of PPE, which also trapped in the emotions. Our eyes desperately tried to communicate the stress, which was only released when, at the end of a shift, alone, we changed out of our scrubs into civilian clothes.

Surprisingly, as a healthcare worker, what worries me most is that as we look back on the waves of Covid-19, we are traumatized, not by the fact that so many people died, but by the way we let them die alone.

15

Keeping Alive the Spirit of Artisanship

Vijay Maitri, Volunteer and Resident of
Kathputli Colony, Delhi

Editors' Note

The global pandemic severely hit those who form the backbone of our cultural heritage—our artisans. In the best of times, they survive on their daily wages, which is always uncertain. For the past fifty years, 2800 families at Kathputli Colony have somehow managed to make their ends meet with frequent challenges. They were now pushed to a state where affording even two meals a day became a mammoth task. The job of a performing artist involves an audience. However, with lockdowns, social distancing and orders banning a gathering of more than fifty people, seeing a crowd anytime soon is a bleak possibility. The coronavirus has severely impaired their functioning, not just temporarily but in the long run as well.

Vijay Maitri is one of the volunteers who stepped up to help the dying Kathputli Colony and its people. From merely volunteering to stirring a full-fledged campaign, he uplifted the spirits and also the livelihoods of the artisans. His story gives an insight into the initial challenges faced, the role of the government and the future of the Kathputli Colony.

*

I am an activist and theatre performer who has been campaigning for the rights of the Kathputli Colony since I was twenty-three (nearly seven years now). The Kathputli Colony in northeast Delhi is my home; it is a ten-minute walk from the Shadipur metro station—a makeshift colony and temporary shelter for a settlement of 10,000 artists, including world-famous puppeteers, magicians, drummers, jugglers, folk dancers, folk singers and acrobats. That's where the colony gets its name from—the kathputliwalas (puppeteers). It is also home to many carpenters, mechanics and daily-wage workers as well. Many artists from Kathputli Colony have been invited to weddings and international cultural fairs to represent India. Currently, there are 2,800 families officially living here.

For a while now, the artisan community has been a dying industry, on its last leg. On average, performers earn their daily wage from various events and acts they perform. How much they make in a day varies greatly, depending on the number of tourists and the tips received on a particular day. On good days, earnings could go up to 1000–2000 rupees; on bad days, it could also be as low as 400–500 rupees. Thus, a layer of uncertainty has always permeated the artists' lives.

And then came Covid-19.

When the nationwide lockdown was announced, Kathputli Colony, once a hub of tourist activities, turned into a small transit camp. About four days into the lockdown, I started getting distress calls from residents of the colony: they were helpless, unable to afford a single meal. One family was holding on to a packet of biscuits, carefully calculating how to divvy up the six pieces to stave off hunger for just a little bit longer.

We began to hear about other slums around the country as well. None seemed as adversely affected as Dharavi, Asia's largest slum, located in India's commercial capital, Mumbai. Dharavi is reportedly one of the world's most congested shanty towns; social distancing is not a luxury people can afford there. And density is a friend of Covid-19. Imagine more than 650,000 people spread over 2.5 grubby sq km, less than a square mile, eight to ten people living together in poky 100 sq ft dwellings, with most residents using community toilets. Homes and factories coexist in single buildings lining the slum's narrow lanes. Most people are informal daily-wage workers who don't cook at home and go out to get their food. This sprawling slum in the heart of Mumbai has received vast amounts of media attention, including for being the inspiration for the Oscar-winning film *Slumdog Millionaire*. Business-school researchers and city planners from around the world have studied its US$1 bn informal economy and urban dynamics.

In Kathputli Colony too, each family lives in a small one-room house, with the roof made of lightweight Aerocon panels, at risk of collapsing at any moment. Everyone shares the community bathrooms, and toilets have irregular, or sometimes no, water supply. Fifteen tankers come once a day to provide water for over 2,000 families, turning the artists into ugly scavengers who have to shove each other out of the way to ensure that they manage to get a small amount of water. The stampede for such fundamental basics leaves permanent scars between already beleaguered communities. And with only a five-litre plastic barrel of water to share within the family, it's not difficult to imagine that they compromise on taking turns to bathe each week.

Unlike Dharavi, however, Kathputli Colony does not enjoy much media attention and is nowhere near as well known. The result of this disparity in popularity? In Dharavi, responding to the Covid-19 crisis, private doctors joined the fever camps. Kathputli Colony, on the other hand, has received barely any medical assistance. The cash-rich municipality, politicians, and non-profits have provided tens of thousands of free meals and rations to most families in Dharavi. Here, we are struggling to afford two meals a day. Bollywood actors and businesses have donated gear, oxygen cylinders, gloves, masks, medicines and ventilators to Dharavi. At Kathputli Colony, various politicians and municipality workers have paid cursory visits, looked at our condition and made big promises—only to forget all about it the moment they walked away.

In the past, when a foreign delegation or VIP guests visited India, Kathputli Colony would be the go-to place to showcase the rich cultural talent the country had to offer. Yet, when it came to saving the craft and the spirit of craftsmanship, no one cared enough. When put into perspective, I can't help but wonder: What if Kathputli Colony and other slum areas in the country had received the kind of attention Dharavi did?

On 26 March 2020, the government unveiled a Rs 1.70 lakh crore economic package for the poor, which included free food grain and cooking gas. This package was to provide for three months as one-time doles to women and poor senior citizens, higher wages to workers, and measures to boost the liquidity of employees. Positive reactions from people across the country started pouring in immediately after Finance Minister Nirmala Sitharaman announced the package. Prime Minister Narendra Modi announced that the Pradhan Mantri Garib Kalyan Package will go a long way in ensuring the food and livelihood security of the poor. 'It is our firm resolve that the poor and vulnerable get all possible help to cope with the testing times,' the PM tweeted.

A close friend of mine, Raju, belongs to the Jatav community, a Dalit caste. He sells lemons and chillies outside a Kali temple, which people string together on their door frames to "ward off evil". Raju's daughters are ragpickers. After the lockdown was announced, none of them could step out to work, since their work doesn't qualify as "essential services". Of all that was sanctioned to them, they could only avail 1 kg of dal and 5 kg of rice per month. For a family of four, a kilo of dal boiled with a tad-more-than-recommended amount of water can last three or four days.

Kathputli Colony has always been regarded as a repository of Indian culture and art. Yet, India has failed to come through for us during these turbulent times—when we perhaps needed it the most. While it is not possible for any individual to fix the situation single-handedly, it is possible to help, to reach out wherever one can—whether as an individual or in groups.

In Kathputli Colony, a few leaders, including me, held a meeting soon after the lockdown was announced. We made a list of those in the colony that are the most vulnerable, names totalling up to almost 700. We then made a realistic assessment of what it would cost us to get them rations—cooking oil, grain, dal and veggies. It adds up to Rs 3,000 per family for a month; for 700 people, that's Rs 21 lakhs. A significant amount by any stretch of the imagination. So, we campaigned to raise the money ... but that would be a long and hard process. To get us started, I, along with a couple of friends, pooled in around Rs 10,000 and purchased basic food supplies. We distributed them to the families who were in dire need. Despite our good intentions, people would hurl abuses at us for favouring select families. It was hard to explain to them why, even amongst the poor, the resource crunch was forcing us to serve those who almost literally had nothing. Even a hard choice as one between buying masks or food, in the end, does have an answer, even if a rather unfortunate one: If one dies of starvation, what good is a mask?

When it became apparent that no external help was coming our way, we decided to devote all our hours into reaching out to both government and non-government organisations for any kind of support and donations. Youngsters started coming into my makeshift office and asking how they could help. With time, things fell into place and our method became more organised. We expanded our reach to fellow artists in Narela, Ghaziabad, Faridabad, Laxmi Nagar, and people living in neighbourhood slums. Presently, we are a team of over 100 volunteers and we received support from organisations such as the Goonj, Azim Premji foundation, Tata Trust, etc.

Gradually, a small initiative became a full-fledged campaign ... our help reached almost 700 families, and eventually, the entire colony along with the neighbourhood. We distributed around 4,348 kits for approximately 12,000 people. While distributing masks and sanitisers in addition to food and necessary groceries, we realised that we were missing an equally important essential good—sanitary pads. The women of the colony told us of their requirements, and in response, we began distributing sanitary pads as well. Eventually, we began producing them on our own, with the help of a few female volunteers.

When we started our relief work, I found out that a lot of people wanted to contribute. But considering that I had never led a fundraising campaign before or knew how to go about it, I was slightly apprehensive. But thankfully, over the years, I was mentored by some great people such as the founder of Goonj, Mr Anshu Gupta, as well as Mr Prakhar Bhartiya, the co-founder of Indian School of Democracy. They walked me through the process and gave me a starting point for my project. I, along with the initial fifty volunteers, decided that we had to set up a system for the inflow of donations.

To kickstart our fundraising programme, we started small within the community itself. Slowly, we realised that people were willing to support. Therefore, in one of our meetings, I suggested that we create a public crowdfunding page. That way, anyone could access the page, read up about our aim and contribute. Since I had the greatest number of contacts within the team, I began sharing the page to my friends and supporters who knew my work. The response was amazing. People started donating in large numbers and that's when the fundraising actually started. Watching the money come in, we immediately increased the quality of our safety kits and medical appliances.

Word started spreading and an article featured on *The Quint* about the Kathputli Colony which worked really well for us as it reached out to the government and millennials who had the means to support. The article had a link that informed the readers of where they could donate and through that link, we got a great response. While media coverage carried the word to the government, garnering NGO attention wasn't difficult. Since I was already collaborating with them on many occasions, I could directly reach out to them for their help. There was a level of trust that they bestowed upon my work which made the whole process a lot easier and barely took any convincing. We then reached out to local MLAs and MPs in Delhi through our donors who had contacts. In addition, we organised online talks and performances to also get attention.

With our dogged efforts and monetary help from NGOs, things have stabilised to a great extent in Kathputli Colony. But how long can this be sustained? How long can non-profits continue to help as they start to run out of resources in what promises to be a long and weary battle? And even after the world comes to a new normal, the future will not be restored for us as quickly as it might for more privileged communities. Here, talented magicians and jugglers have taken to doing odd jobs and selling biryani on the street to earn a living. When the pandemic finally exits, will these artisans be able to go back to doing what they loved, given the economic uncertainty of doing so?

After the first wave subsided, there was slight relief in the air but also an important realisation. During the initial days, the atmosphere in the colony saw desperation and quarrels mainly as an outcome of fear. People were insecure but soon, they realised that this is something that is bigger than all of us. No one was coming to their rescue and they had to make huge decisions in order to sustain their livelihood. As a result, once the unlock began, many artisans started migrating to different states in search of work. Although their forte was art, they began work in construction sites and other daily-wage jobs. Everyone wanted to earn money.

The first lockdown created immense mental pressure on the artisans. So far, there have been nineteen deaths in Kathputli. Out of those, seven were suicides. One can imagine the kind of mental pressure one was going through. However, the official figures state only two deaths.

Before the onset of the second wave, when weddings resumed, many drummers made a quick buck but that was it. Other puppeteers and performers weren't getting any work. We tried to set up stalls, conduct workshops and approached institutions for online performances. While some institutions agreed and we were able to support thirty-two artists, this was not a long-term sustainable solution. The pandemic taught us to adapt and go digital. The future is digital and the past year has only reinforced this belief. Hence, we've started training artisans on how to use zoom, Instagram reels and other online methods to showcase their art. For now, we are trying to utilise their talent and gain a digital footprint for the same. We wish to expand and introduce stitching projects for women, allowing them to make masks using reusable cloth for various NGOs.

Another focus of our efforts is children. They have been silent sufferers of this pandemic. Since their schools were closed and many did not have means of attending online classes, small kids ventured into procuring and selling drugs. It breaks my heart to see their precious childhood take such a turn. We are working on setting up small learning centres called Jagriti for children who are unable to attend schools and do not have resources for online schooling.

A year on, I would still say that the situation is not great. There are still families who are only able to afford one-time meals. We all hoped for it to get better but insecurity continues to loom. The fear of death remains. I like to believe that the community survived the disease not because they could practise social distancing or double masking or sanitisation, it was purely because of our immunity system. Since we've always been living in unhygienic conditions with foul air, unclean water and among densely populated areas, our bodies naturally have more immunity than the average Indian living in high-rise apartments.

In the six years I have worked for Kathputli Colony, I have never seen anything quite like this. People often ask me why I quit my job and risked my life to help others in the colony. The answer is simple: these people are family. Kathputli Colony has always seen struggle and systemic indifference, but what I've seen during this pandemic is beyond comprehension. Having said that, I also know that I cannot lose hope. Helping my community get through these trying times is the only thing that gets me out of bed every morning, making me come to work just to see the smiles and a sense of hope on people's faces. I do not want to let those smiles fade away.

The war is not yet over.

16

It's All in Your Head until It Happens

Karan Bhangay, Covid-19 Survivor,
Serial Entrepreneur, Owner of Multiple Start-ups under the Global Luxury Group

Editors' Note

One of the factors that make Covid-19 scarier than other diseases with similar mortality rates is the wide range of symptoms it manifests. The disease can be mild or moderate to severe and life-threatening across people, with older people at a higher risk of mortality. During the original 2019 wave, the most common symptoms included fever, dry cough and fatigue. The loss or distortion of the senses of smell and taste has become one of the unique identifiers of the virus. However, many people present with "atypical" symptoms as well, often less obviously connected to a disease primarily understood as a respiratory disease. This makes it much harder for the person to suspect that they have the virus and allows the disease to go undetected and untested, thereby increasing the risk of transmission.

For instance, many were affected only by gastrointestinal symptoms, such as nausea, vomiting, diarrhoea and generalised abdominal pain. A November 2020 study by the Faculty of Medicine and Dentistry in University of Alberta found that almost 20 per cent of Covid-19 patients only show gastrointestinal symptoms, i.e., one in five people would not show the most commonly associated Covid-19 symptoms. "Seeing these things is not necessarily telling us a patient has Covid-19," said Mitch Wilson, radiologist and clinical lecturer, Faculty of Medicine and Dentistry, University of Alberta. "It could be from a variety of potential causes. But one of those potential causes is infection from the virus, and in an environment where Covid-19 is very prevalent, it's something to consider and potentially raise as a possibility to the referring physician." Similarly, some Covid-19 positive patients presented only with ocular issues such as conjunctivitis. Several cases have been reported in which RT-PCR testing on tears have demonstrated the presence of the virus. An NCBI study found evidence that in some cases conjunctivitis may occur as a sole manifestation of Covid-19.

The crisis is exacerbated by the fact that a large percentage of the population remains asymptomatic while infected with the virus, making them silent carriers. Early during the pandemic, research suggested that this could be as high as 81 per cent. This creates a situation where everyone who has not been tested and ruled out as negative must be treated as carrying the virus. Moreover, findings also indicate that being asymptomatic does not exclude the patient from the negative impact of the virus and that the infection could still be causing harm despite the lack of any outward signs. Data now shows that asymptomatic as well as symptomatic patients can sustain long-term damage and injuries. Even in those who do not succumb to the infection, post-recovery, there are increased risks of fatal complications such as clotting in addition to organ damage to the lungs, kidney, heart and brain. According to the Centre for Disease Control and Prevention (CDC), the most common lasting symptoms are fatigue, shortness of breath, cough, joint pain and chest pain. Other issues include cognitive problems, difficulty concentrating, depression, muscle pain, headache, rapid heartbeat and intermittent fever.

For those asymptomatic people who never get tested, the risks go undetected until a complication arises. "It's a very big portion of people, and although they are silent without symptoms, internally, they are taking hits in there, inside their body so they don't even know it," says Eric Topol, MD. Across four different studies of people with asymptomatic infections, the lung CT scans of 50 per cent showed ground glass opacities. Valentina Puntmann, MD, an expert in heart imaging at the University Hospital Frankfurt, Germany, and her team of researchers scanned the hearts of 100 patients who had recently recovered from Covid-19, including eighteen who were asymptomatic. While not all of the asymptomatic patients had markers for heart damage, the few who did had some of the highest levels measured in the study. In some instances, individuals developed neurological symptoms such as brain fog, headaches and insomnia, and an increased susceptibility to postural orthostatic tachycardia syndrome, or POTS.

Being a new virus, the Covid-19 remains vastly understudied. According to medical professionals, what we do know might barely scratch the surface, and the long-term implications of the disease are yet to be understood. Researchers are still looking into how and why the virus affects different people in such a variety of ways, with some people showing no short-term or long-term damage, some showing only short-term damage, and others sustaining life-threatening organ damage or disabilities. As of now, says Topol, "Who knows what other organs are being affected? We don't know. No one's ever looked."

Asymptomatic sufferers of the disease became unwitting carriers, spreading the disease further. Symptomless transmission has been one of the most insidious aspects of the pandemic, not only making the virus harder to fight but also putting the ones asymptomatically affected in a compromising and confused position. In India, this situation has been compounded by the shortage of testing.

Even as lockdowns lifted and people emerged from their home quarantine, they had to reconcile with and navigate a world not yet ready to welcome them back into a still cautious society. While federal health experts and epidemiologists agreed that patients who were asymptomatic and tested negative no longer pose risk of infection to others, some people were still confronted with a fear-driven stigma from the outside world.

Statistically, the age demographic most vulnerable to Covid-19 and associated mortality is the older population. However, contrary to public perception, it is not deadly only to those above sixty. About 70 per cent patients of Covid-19 are forty and above. Among those that succumbed to the virus in 2020, 35 per cent were recorded in the age group of 45–60 years, 10 per cent in the age group of 26–44 years, and 1 per cent each in the age group of 18–25 years and below 17 years, according to Health Secretary Rajesh Bhushan. While this makes younger people less susceptible to Covid-19 related mortality, it certainly does not make them risk-free.

Further, in the second wave in India, a marginal increase was recorded in the number of young people testing positive for the virus along with an increase in the positivity rate, with the mutant strains seemingly more infectious and more lethal. India's double mutant strain—the B.1.617—has also hit the younger population particularly hard, even those without comorbidities. "While earlier it was believed that Covid-19 afflicts mostly the elderly having comorbidities, this is no more the case. We see a lot of young patients (not children) with bad pneumonia. I think it is the mutant strain," said Dr S.M. Bandekar, dean of Goa Medical College. WHO describes it as a "variant of interest" and that the mutations may make the virus more transmissible and cause more severe disease or evade vaccine immunity.

In several states, doctors say they are seeing more young patients than they did last year. "October and November had mostly elderly people, now it is mostly people in their 30s," says Dr Sumit Ray, head of department for critical care medicine at Holy Family Hospital. According to a government official in Chhattisgarh, more younger patients are being infected, and more severely than last year. "We are seeing more deaths among those who are above thirty years, more deaths of those without comorbidities." Whether this is due to the overall increase in the number of cases in the country, insufficient vaccination among younger people, or the mutant strains themselves remains to be seen.

A combination of complacency, both among the public and the government, slow production and distribution of vaccines, and the missed opportunity to fortify the healthcare system, made the second wave of Covid-19 more devastating. The mutant variants spread faster, and may be, according to WHO, "potentially resistant to vaccine protection", causing even vaccinated people to pick up the virus, rendering the vaccination drive less effective than it would have been several months ago. WHO Chief Scientist Soumya Swaminathan says, "In a large country like India, you could have transmission at low levels ... At that point it's very hard to suppress, because it's then involving tens of thousands of people and it's multiplying at a rate at which it's very difficult to stop." She further says that vaccination, while crucial, may not be enough to control the outbreak, since it might take "months, if not years" to inoculate 70 to 80 per cent of the country's population of more than 130 crore.

In India, the devastation of the second wave was made infinitely worse by a healthcare system that all but collapsed—there was a rampant shortage of beds, oxygen and even medication. There were reports of people dying outside hospitals, while waiting for oxygen beds or ICU admittance. Social media swarmed with heart-wrenching appeals for oxygen cylinders, plasma donation and medications such as Remdesivir. Yet, even in a situation as bleak and hopeless as this, all was not lost.

In response to public and private appeals for resources, many came forward to compile information regarding the availability of medicines and other requirements. Recovered individuals signed up in mass numbers to donate plasma for the experimental treatment that may help aid recovery in severely affected patients. Many people and families took it upon themselves to provide meals and essentials to quarantined folks at minimal cost or for free. Social media was used rigorously to amplify appeals and many people managed to get critical care at odd hours—in the form of hospital beds, life-saving drugs, oxygen—thanks to the empathy of virtual strangers. Companies and for-profit organisations too stepped up, with some brands donating 100 per cent of their proceeds to Covid-19 relief. For instance, Pickrr Technologies, an Indian logistics tech start-up, announced a 100 per cent subsidy on delivery charges for all non-profit organisations supplying Covid-19 essentials in India. According to a CSRBOX report that analysed responses by large companies/corporates in India, BSE/NSE listed companies have contributed 37 per cent share in funding towards Covid-19, followed by private companies at 20 per cent. Additionally, CSR foundations are helping hospitals and frontline health workers, ensuring adequate supply of medicines, protective and safety gear and equipment. Religious organisations, too, have joined in, with mandirs, gurudwaras, masjids and churches being converted to makeshift hospitals.

The fight is far from over. As doctors and scientists anticipate future waves, it is important to remember how at a time of such pandemonium, people have come together in large numbers to be kind to each other and to help one another through this crisis, when it would perhaps be understandable if, preoccupied with their own well-being, they had less empathy for strangers.

Karan Bhangay, a start-up entrepreneur and a Covid-19 survivor, shares his experience of contracting the virus, along with its physical and emotional aftermath. Karan is part of the pool of entrepreneurs who conduct most business affairs offline. For people like him, meeting various people from across the country is an instrumental part of their professional life. This is an unfiltered and honest account of his experience, how he conducted business, managed daily chores, kept his life running—all the while living alone, and infected by a virus that continued to ravage the world.

*

By the time India was fully under the shadow of the pandemic, I knew as much about Covid-19 as the guy next door, which was quite a lot, given the constant stream of information about the virus on every media platform.

But did I think I could get it? Honestly, no. I was distanced from the thought of getting infected. I mean, it was possible, but … *how could I get it, right*? Like all sensible people, I was following all the necessary precautions—wearing masks, using hand sanitiser, washing hands, social distancing.

Moreover, the virus was said to be deadly to those above sixty. Research showed that healthy millennials who contracted Covid-19 had a great chance of survival. While these are only statistical odds, subconsciously, I felt that the virus wasn't a huge threat to me personally. I was young, healthy and had a strong immune system.

For me, the virus was out there in the world. Therefore, I didn't entertain the idea that I could get it.

Until I did.

A Comedy of Errors

I was heading to the mall to run some errands. The security guards were following the standard protocol and checked my Covid-19 status on Aarogya Setu—an Indian app that allows for contact tracing, syndromic mapping and self-assessment. It alerts you if you are surrounded by any potential covid-positive patients. If the status on the app reads "you are safe", the security guards let you in. Aware of this procedure, I stood in the queue, waiting for my turn to enter the mall. The guard asked to check my phone, and I handed it to him without looking at it.

"Sir, you cannot enter the mall. Please immediately step aside, and I request you to not touch anything or anyone. Move, immediately!"

Baffled by this sudden, unexpected behaviour, I looked at my phone. To my utter horror, the screen was red, and it said, "You are Covid-19 positive."

This could not be happening!

The entire management at the mall came running to the ground floor and people around me were in shock. It felt as though I had committed a crime and everyone's eyes were fixated on me. The manager asked me to leave immediately and inform authorities in my area that I had contracted the virus. I did as they told me, but none of it made any sense. How was I positive? I hadn't even got myself tested yet. After making a gazillion phone calls to Aarogya Setu, I realised that someone in Hyderabad had made the careless mistake of feeding in the wrong number. The result of this minor error cost me big time. On paper, I became infected with Covid-19, even though in reality, I was fine.

Within the next two to three hours, the word had spread like wildfire in my society: Karan *has* Covid-19. I did what a patient is expected to do without trying to convince everyone around me that I was, in fact, hale and hearty. For nearly a month, I stayed home with *fake* Covid-19.

Despite the strange ordeal, however, the fact that I was not really sick kept me sane and going. Once the drama died down, I could finally venture out again. I had a small get-together at my bachelor pad with six of my friends. We played poker, ate pizza, watched cricket, and called it a day.

A couple of nights later, I suddenly felt very tired and feverish. I slept the whole day and woke up around 2 a.m. with an irritable itch in my throat. I wasn't really alarmed; I made myself warm *kaada*, had a tablet of Dolo and Azithromycin as my doctor had recommended for any mild fever or cold and went back to bed. The next morning, I felt much better, although still fatigued. I ordered pizza for lunch, had my medicines again and slept for another six hours.

With everything that had happened before, the thought that I could be infected with Covid-19—for real this time—did cross my mind. But I tried not to dwell on it. Fortunately, testing facilities were available in my society. To be doubly sure and rid myself of the nagging psychological baggage, I decided to get tested.

A long line of people waited for their turn, and I could see all my friends standing there, the ones who were in my house the other day playing poker. Confused but relieved to see known faces, I patiently waited for my turn. After the collection of nasal and throat swabs, I was asked to wait for my results. As I waited, I saw a few uncles and aunties stare at me and exchange glances, clearly talking about me.

After a short wait, a lady came out of the testing facility and quietly told me, "You are Covid-19 positive. Without causing any anxiety among the people here, I request you to go back to your house right away."

As instructed, I did not react and immediately started racing towards my house. As I entered my house and locked the door from inside, I felt like I was being sucked into a vacuum. I had so many things planned for the days ahead, and I could see them fade away—my job, my routine, my social life.

My mind was occupied with a series of "What ifs". What if I don't get better soon? What if my symptoms get *more* serious day by day? What if … I *don't* make it? I suddenly remembered the thirty-one-year-old man who had collapsed outside the hospital in Hyderabad. The knowledge that I was positive burst my bubble of security. I was young, yes, but with this virus, anything was possible. *It's not like no young person had died.* Staying alone in complete isolation only added to this gloom. When you are left alone with your thoughts, your voice is all that you hear; it is the only perspective that surrounds you.

That night, I sat down and began writing names of the people who were important in my life, people with whom I needed to make amends, people I've let down, people I'm grateful for, people I've hurt, people I need to communicate with, people with whom I have unresolved conflicts. Faces of my parents, sister and friends flashed before my eyes. Those seventeen days of quarantine were poignant; they changed my outlook and approach to life. I saw a significant shift in my relationship with my parents and sister. Family's love is often taken for granted because, after all, family sticks around no matter what. But it is only times like these that allow one to see things that are often overlooked. Not only my family but also my friends … the love and concern I received in this dark phase of life was overwhelming. In many ways, it kept me sane and got me through the whole thing.

My sister, living in Los Angeles, could only do so much from another continent. Yet, she managed to take care of everything

I needed without me even telling her about it. Medicines, immunity boosters, groceries—she found a way to send them to me. From Hyderabad, my parents ensured that the physical distance did not affect the emotional bond between us. From sharing recipes to checking up every now and then, they did not let me feel alone for a single moment.

Even my neighbours and people in the society did everything they could. Being a bachelor and living alone comes with the big fat burden of cooking all your meals. In a pre-Covid-19 world, Swiggy and Zomato were my best friends. Now, I had to figure out how to cook three meals a day, all by myself, while also being sick. I put out a request on the society WhatsApp group for people to drop off food in case they had prepared extra or had any leftovers. I didn't expect much, but figured it was worth a shot. To my surprise, I began receiving delicious meals almost immediately, for both lunch and dinner. Every day, someone would ring the bell and leave the food outside for me. Such gestures may not be grand in isolation, but collectively, they eradicated all my gloom. Despite being sucked into a dark place after first learning that I was infected, I was now coming out stronger. The experience also left a deep and lasting impact on me, and positively affected everything I did from here on out.

Instead of killing me as I had feared, Covid-19 gave me a new lease on life in many ways.

I decided to exercise this newfound positivity and energy in all areas of life. Once my quarantine ended and I no longer had symptoms, I decided to donate my plasma for plasma therapy. It is a medical process through which recovered patients of the virus donate their blood to create antibodies to fight the infection. After I was examined, the doctor confirmed that my antibodies count was 25, an impressive count that would help them immensely if I donated my blood. Without any hesitation, I signed up immediately, coming out with nothing but gratitude.

Before this ordeal, I had followed the usual path to success—focusing on money, career, goals and ambition—a linear path with no scope for digression if I had to make it big. However, I now take things slow, living one day at a time, no longer obsessed about planning ahead. All of 2020 proved to me that plans don't mean much in the face of greater issues. We give so much importance to rigid plans, but at the end of the day, they are uncertain and vulnerable to change. Living is not about reaching an end goal. It is about savouring the moments, knowing that life is fragile and fleeting, which only makes it all the more beautiful.

17

A Symbiosis of Solidarity

Vidya Yeravdekar, Pro-chancellor,
Symbiosis International University

Editors' Note

The coronavirus pandemic came as a greater systemic shock to the education sector at large. The whole model of education relies heavily on collaboration and experiential learning. The coronavirus forced campuses to shut down indefinitely.

College and university leaders have had to tackle logistical, economic and psychological impacts. From significant, potentially unparalleled, declines in enrolment to ensuring safety of students living on campus, university owners across the world are making a wave of decisions in response to the crisis. Decisions that could profoundly alter the landscape of higher education for years to come.

Among the most prominent issues, students are expressing grave dissatisfaction with how the virus has changed the nature of academic institutions. To some, online classes and closed student centres, gyms and science labs do not seem worth the high prices they are paying. International students aren't expressing interest in admissions because of travel restrictions and concerns about studying abroad.

Wealthy universities have begun announcing austerity measures: buffering their losses, freezing salaries, slow academic hiring, suspending discretionary spending and looking for other budget cuts.

Vidya Yeravdekar, the principal director of Symbiosis Society, shares how the university is growing from strength to strength in the face of an unprecedented global crisis. Symbiosis's journey with education spans five decades. Catering to over 30,000 students from more than eighty-one countries and from all over India, Yeravdekar talks about spearheading the effort towards stabilising the situation on campus.

From adjusting to online classes to ensuring safe home-bound journeys of the students, here's how one of the oldest universities in the world innovated in a turbulent time.

*

The ongoing pandemic has transfigured individual and collective realities for the foreseeable future and has made us reflect upon our earlier existence with both nostalgia and criticism. The motto of Symbiosis is *Vasudhaiva Kutumbakam*, meaning that the world is one big family. Interestingly, this principle upon which the university has thrived for fifty years is what this pandemic has also gone on to accentuate—the world is indeed one big family. It has also brought with it transformations, some of which we are only beginning to understand, while others have led us to reacknowledge our innate capacity to negate uncertainty through resolve, creativity and cohesion.

The day-to-day challenges that have suddenly emerged as a consequence—the restrictions of movement, logistical issues and inaccessibility to critical resources, among countless others—have caught most of us off guard. And since the pandemic is now a global phenomenon, it has become harder to draw a line between self-preservation and social responsibility. Even a small oversight, such as forgetting to wear a mask while out for a walk, can potentially have mass-scale implications. Similarly, efforts that are born out of a sense of community can have a profound influence on the sense of self.

My father, S.B. Mujumdar, dreamt of creating a "home away from home" in an environment where groups of people from various cultural backgrounds could mutually benefit from one another. That dream is what we call Symbiosis today. We are a family of academic institutions with over 40,000 Indian and international students on campus. This year marks the fiftieth year since inception; however, the celebration brought with it consternation, in the form of a global pandemic.

I vividly remember that when the nationwide lockdown was announced, the immediate attention of the staff went in ensuring the health and safety of the students. A majority of the student body comes from outside the city of Pune. Thus, not only did we have international students, but also students from many different cities in India. At that point, one critical question emerged: how do we safely send over 40,000 students back home amidst a pandemic? A significant section of the students come from underprivileged backgrounds and do not have the means to book a flight home. Similarly, the challenge for international students was two-fold as they had to fly to another country all together. Rules and regulations for each country were different and some countries had temporarily disallowed any overseas travel.

The task force that was established could only identify problems one after the other with no solution in sight. So, we decided to tackle each problem one by one. Something I was conscious of throughout was that the safety of students took precedence, and at no cost could we compromise on that.

Hence, procedures to evacuate students from the campus were immediately put in place. Many of the administrative staff members who were tasked with ensuring this process were retired army personnel. Since they were trained in crisis management, this proved to be of great advantage. I had complete faith that our students were in good hands. They were compassionate towards the students, not only in terms of providing food or medical assistance, but also while offering mental support. With a palpable sense of panic setting around, it was essential to restore calmness—especially in the minds of the students. They were away from home and unaware about the impact that the situation could have on their academic life, or how long this would last. Looking at the plight of our students, we also extended assistance by providing food grains, groceries and other essential amenities to foreign students who were stranded in other universities in Pune. At a time like this, the administrative staff really stepped up and got things under control.

Upon implementing the primary set of measures, the next challenge was to tackle academics. Virtual classes had to be conducted with the same academic rigour, interest and efficiency as expected from a conventional classroom. While I was witnessing the digitisation of education, I was also aware of the opportunity cost of the same. Experiential learning has proven to be effective for a number of reasons.

People enjoy going to colleges not only for the learning aspect, but because it effectuates holistic growth in individuals, and they gain from being exposed to an environment that fosters interactions with people from different cultural and socio-economic backgrounds. It is about networking, learning to live together in hostels, and being culturally sensitive to those who are less privileged. Therefore, these form crucial elements of growth that digital learning cannot substitute as yet. But in order to ensure that education doesn't come to a standstill, the university, like other academic institutions around the world, had to make the transition to online learning.

In my opinion, the switch to digital learning happened as more of a reaction than a proactive measure. Earlier, the faculty members would use digital tools as a supplement but never considered it to be the primary method for imparting knowledge. For example, services like Zoom had existed before as well, but because the situation never demanded it, we rarely ventured into experimenting with them. But fortunately, or unfortunately, the pandemic brought about a situation where there was a critical need to adapt. That is precisely why things are certainly different now. The whole of March and April 2020 were devoted to making a smooth changeover to online learning. Despite certain initial hiccups, the ongoing academic session was successfully completed online.

Once the summer breaks began, it gave the educators a couple of months to take a more charged approach towards digital learning. There was finally sufficient time to assess various tools of technology and for conducting online workshops for the faculty. The aim was to equip them with an online way of functioning for the next semester, and possibly, for the near term. Another huge aspect of digital learning which required consideration was the inaccessibility of the Internet to a large number of students. There are also network and bandwidth issues in certain locations of the country. However, the two-month window gave enough time to adapt to these challenges.

Having been at the forefront of watching the educational sector transform, I've also witnessed the positive consequences that accompany this pandemic. It has certainly broadened the scope of communication. Before we were hit with Covid-19, approaching experts and faculty members from overseas universities for lectures in our campus was a complicated task. There were a lot of factors one had to consider, mostly logistical. Any important meeting required me to fly to another city. But now, within a fraction of a second, we can achieve all these tasks over Zoom or any virtual platform. The variables to consider have decreased significantly, with less issues and equal efficiency.

Moreover, it has initiated a whole new world of Collaborative Online International Learning (COIL), which is a system that connects accredited courses, and links classrooms of two or more higher education institutions from different parts of the world. Faculties from two cultures/countries work together to develop a shared syllabus, emphasising the importance of collaborative learning. These are mechanisms that you would often hear about in workshops and consider promising, but then eventually forget. However, they are finally being implemented now and it is possible to see the internationalisation of higher education.

Looking back, one thing I can say with surety is that there is always light at the end of the tunnel. What we have displayed during the pandemic is global solidarity. Be it academic institutions, the corporate sector, or healthcare workers, this is the coming together of people in a way like never before. I cannot speak for other sectors, but the future of education is undoubtedly reliant on collaboration. This pandemic has made it apparent that one cannot work in isolation. Everyone's intent of producing a Covid-19 vaccine can only become reality when collaboration and teamwork are at play. The same principle can be applied across platforms. As far as education is concerned, it is about interdependence rather than being independent. Educational institutions are seeing an evolution and gearing towards a wholesome blend of conventional methods with digital and in-person learning, and a completely new vertical of online delivery of education is imminent. Our vision may be restricted to what we see today, but there is a larger force at play, determining actions for the future. What we are seeing is a symbiosis of minds, and a reiteration of the idea of *Vasudhaiva Kutumbakam*.

18

A 152-year-old Legacy, Upended by Covid-19

Nonita Kalra, Editor-in-chief, *TataCLiQ Luxury*
Former Editor, *Harper's Bazaar India*

Editors' Notes

Fashion magazines are vehicles for luxury fantasies. They sell readers on consumerist dreams. The coronavirus pandemic and the lockdown have derailed those dreams. As a result, fashion magazines have been derailed both in production and purpose. It's not just that. The year 2020 is set to be the worst year in the history of the modern luxury business, with supply chains in free-fall and media advertising budgets slashed. It's not just that shoppers have stopped shopping, or that fewer people in the fashion industry, from seamstresses to salespeople, are able to go to work, it's that magazines were already a fraught business. It's that many people have been re-evaluating their moral relationship with consumption. And now there's a pandemic to address.

From Condé Nast (the publisher of Vogue, Vanity Fair *and* The New Yorker*), to Vice Media and BuzzFeed, which was* *headed towards profitability in 2020, magazines and digital media companies have been ravaged by the pandemic. The next wave of print stories that come out have to be made with the coronavirus crisis in mind.*

In times like this, the task of being a fashion editor is a constant balancing act. You need to read the room constantly: not just every day, but every hour and minute, registering appetites and anxieties that are constantly changing. Consequently, learning how to run a magazine nimbly on an ever-receding budget has become an essential skill for editors.

Magazines around the world have been exploring different ideas that they might never have thought about or talked about before. From a creative standpoint, editors and publishers are taking advantage of the chaos. They are using this as an excuse to try new things; to shake up familiar visuals and stale formats; to introduce more originality at a time when the line between editorial content and advertising is blurrier than ever.

But the industry isn't willing to declare disaster yet. They should, and are, pivoting. Glossy magazines have had to (finally) stop selling fantasy and reckon with reality. It's complicated; to the extent of questioning: what's the point of a fashion magazine now? In between stories about eye creams and tips on styling a denim jacket, it takes courage to talk about the little things that matter. However, there is also a sort of liberation about it. Nonita Kalra, the former editor-in-chief of Elle India *and* Harper's Bazaar India, *opens up about innovating magazine content in the middle of a worldwide pandemic, maintaining personal and professional discipline, keeping team spirits up, and about her personal and professional innovations during the coronavirus pandemic, the consequent lockdown and everything in between.*

*

When we were hit by the seriousness of the Covid-19 pandemic, we knew a lockdown was imminent, but none of us were expecting it to be announced so immediately. And we certainly didn't think it would carry on for so long. The day we packed our computers and started preparing to work from home, I remember all of us leaving the office silently (the *India Today* office is called Mediaplex, and is situated in Film City, Noida). There was no panic but there was a sense of the unknown. A few days later we officially went into lockdown and stayed that way till the magazine was put on a pause, subsequently.

In the media, you don't get a day off from deadlines. We had a magazine to put to bed, printing schedules to meet, and the next big issue to prep for. The first thing we did was to fix a call every morning and every evening. Personally, I realised the importance of not letting things slide. I am a creature of discipline and habit. I am the sort of person who wakes up at 4 a.m. to workout, clear emails and schedule an agenda for the day. By the time my team starts their workday, they have already received their tasks and to-do lists. I continued the routine throughout the lockdown. For all outward appearances it seemed that everything had changed. But reality only set in by the second lockdown extension, by then we were certain that there would be a third and a fourth one.

To run a successful magazine, you can't work in isolation. You need coherence. Individual effort needs to be aligned cohesively. The fashion team needs to be up-to-date with what the beauty team is doing, and they need to know what the editorial team is working on. It needs to be put out as one seamless conversation. You cannot say that there is a trend of sustainability in fashion, and then be recommending plastic products for beauty. Only when it all comes together is it a movement.

On a typical day at the office, we would meet every morning over an edit meeting, where we drank coffee and ate chocolate. We learnt over the lockdown that we craved this connection. Being able to see each other's faces—even if it was over Zoom—was reassuring. And we stuck to that routine, every single day of the week. As a team, we learnt how to play tag virtually. We also used this time to sit down and reflect. We felt that we had to question the role of the fashion magazine and think about the message we were sending out, particularly during the pandemic. People were not buying clothes, so trends weren't relevant anymore. There was no desire for handbags or shoes. No one was wearing jewellery or makeup. We had stripped down to our bare basics. Even food trends—the fancy croissants, the muffins, the wellness drinks—were all gone. So, the questions facing us were: What is the big picture? How can we stay relevant? What are the stories we need to tell? At this point all magazines and newspapers had ceased printing. However, content was being consumed more than ever, only it was digital. All digital.

That's when we decided we had to continue telling stories, but we could fix everything that we thought was wrong with fashion magazines.

I've been in the business for three decades, and what I love most about fashion magazines is that we treat women's concerns as primary. Essentially, fashion magazines are women's magazines. Newspapers or weekly's like *India Today* only give you the male perspective. No one looks at how women feel. I've always used this avenue as an opportunity to talk about what women want. Either through conversations around health, or how we use clothing as a political statement. I love that beauty comes with the promise of immediate delivery or how powerful the perfect shade of red lipstick can be to a woman in need of a confidence boost.

We put all of these beliefs into our digital communication. It must be remembered that *Bazaar* did not have a website, so we never had a budget for what we had started or were about to do. We had a print budget but that was obviously suspended. So, we kept our idea small, and sweet. With a series that focussed on the "the little things that bring me joy". It came from the "one for sorrow, two for joy" nursery rhyme. It also came from the fact that during the silence of the lockdown we were actually hearing birds again. It was a different world. The skies were blue, the air was clean, noise pollution was down to nothing. We were locked in, but nature was reclaiming its space.

This series exploded. We saw our numbers grow organically, we just stayed true to what was happening in our lives. We started to tell stories about the little things that made us happy: it could be reading a book, spending time with family, eating something simple, finding joy in our favourite black dress. I think what the reader appreciated was that we approached work-from-home in an honest way. There was nothing pretentious or cool about our approach; we were just being honest.

Working from home is not cool, it's about facing who you are. We started getting calls from stars, celebrities, friends of the magazine, asking to be part of this conversation. One of our first covers had actor Janhvi Kapoor without makeup, cuddling her dog, Panda. Shruti Hassan created a special song for the next cover. Aditi Rao Hydari danced for us. Later, we put together all the Indian actors who have gone on to become global stars to appear on one cover—from Rahul Khanna to Jameela Jamil. We even ran a "24 hours with art" series, with twelve covers releasing over a day. The change we effected was that we made it personal. We were able to say that the reader is you and me. I would continually ask my team, "Does this make sense to you? If not, drop it."

We didn't do endless amounts of DIY content, or bake many loaves of banana bread or recommend at-home face masks. Migrant workers didn't have food to eat, and it felt ridiculously self-indulgent to be doing any of that. We, instead, focussed on music and poetry and the things that make us happy (irrespective of class or status).

Any good magazine will listen first. And this is what I always tell my team: Listen. We launched the Bazaar Conscious Beauty Awards, in 2019, because we were hearing that there is a desire to move away from chemical-heavy beauty. This idea was interestingly being spearheaded by women entrepreneurs. We translated this into a movement. That's a magazine's role. The day we forget that, we will have an utterly tone-deaf product.

As a result of the lockdown, we did our first FaceTime shoot. Conducting virtual photoshoots was a liberating experience! The first sense of freedom came from not pushing trends. We were stepping into people's cupboards and truly styling them. Less fashion, more style. That's what *Bazaar* is really about.

Let me give you a little brief on the magazine business. In most markets, *Elle* is the first entrant as it targets women between the ages of eighteen and thirty-five. Its role is to familiarise a reader with fashion. The tone is always instructional and conversational. When I took over *Elle* as the editor-in-chief in 2000, the brief we were given about our reader was that she was an individualistic combination of high street and high fashion. The *Elle* girl would wear Levi's jeans, her grandmother's vintage jacket, ballet shoes from Zara, only her belt might be Burberry. The smallest piece in her wardrobe would be a luxury brand. It is pretty much a reflection of how anyone starts out building a wardrobe. You buy what you can afford. When *Vogue* enters a market, you know there is more money, more knowledge of brands. It is associated with status. That's why it calls itself "The

Bible". *Harper's Bazaar* is for a woman who is more mature, she can be from the early thirties to her fifties. She knows who she is. She gives back to society, she generally is invested in wellness for herself and her family, she buys art. She is sophisticated. She doesn't want trends; she wants the one great buy.

So what does this have to do with our digital journey? Translating these nuances from print to digital can be difficult but for us, making the transition was not difficult; we just stayed true to our nature. If you couldn't go out and buy that classic white shirt, we showed you how to dress it up with your own accessories, from your own collection. We looked within to create a statement. Isn't that the true definition of style?

In the twenty-first century, you would have to be living under a rock if you didn't use Instagram. Or your camera for a selfie. Everyone has hit the video button on their smartphone and recorded some kind of film. So even though we didn't have our own website, the *Bazaar* team was quick to adapt because we had been waiting for a long time to express ourselves digitally. What we didn't expect was how aggressively we would create content. But I guess we were hyper-excited and went for it at breakneck speed. But it was a simple ecosystem born out of everyday realities.

All we did was help tell stories. The ease of this transition made us really ambitious. And personal. We started with shooting models at home, all across the world. And then for *Brides Today* (I was the editor for a year, from 2019 to 2020) we even persuaded actor Athiya Shetty to sift through her mother and grandmother's cupboards and pull out their heirloom pieces. People stepped up and out of their comfort zones because we were all in the most uncomfortable situation of our lives. While we had the privilege of sitting in the safety of our homes, the uncertainty of the virus was nerve-wracking. While it may or may not kill you, it could be fatal for your parents and grandparents. Let's get real, we are still living in a cloud of fear. Creativity was the only thing that would make the sun shine through. At times like this, you are bound to see a cultural renaissance. We also used the time to erase some of the ugliness that we had gifted ourselves. We found meaningful creativity. Tragically, many people will go back to the old ways of consumption. But I am hopeful that the mindset has changed, in some ways, for some people.

This is a year of change. We have little choice in the matter. Change is an inevitable. You can take change and make it ugly and negative or go with the positive. This is the year that has reaffirmed that. I always thought I was an introvert. I've always believed that there's greater value in holding yourself private. Understandably, in our business, if you're seen having friends, people will say that you're playing favourites. But I do miss human contact. I miss the people I love.

When my generation of women started work (I am fifty-two now—will be when the book releases) we made it our primary role. I never wanted a work-life balance, I only wanted work. Perhaps I felt I was fighting a battle for all young women, I wanted them to have the same privileges and rights as me. To be heard, to be taken seriously. I felt it was my responsibility because I had had the privilege. I was successful in my own right, I was able to do what I wanted, to travel, spend my own money. Now, post-Covid-19, I think it's going to be so fun to have a personal life. This pandemic has taught me that we are nothing without human relationships. We need our hugs. I want to reach out to people and say "you are okay". I am also allowing myself to be kinder to me.

I think it's hard for any of us to switch off. Our homes have become the place where we work, where we sleep, the place of all battles, and all our victories. But it is equally important to step out. To create your own identity and voice. How can we manage this while we are still largely housebound? By making time for ourselves. I still wake up and work out. During this period, I started virtual Kathak classes with Sufi dancer Manjari Chaturvedi. That was my gift to myself. The sound of ghungroos, dancing, using your body, whirling, elevates you. For a Type-A personality, liberation doesn't come in a book or a movie, because all of that is work for me. I'm hyperkinetic and that's my favourite state to be in. I just want to run, run, run, do, do, do! In some ways this year has been wonderfully liberating as well. It all depends on how you want to review it. How you choose to live it.

19

The Covid-19 Bulletin Is Here to Stay

Surbhi R. Sharma, Journalist and Anchor, India TV

Editors' Note

In times of unprecedented chaos, the world often turns to newspapers and news channels for immediate and reliable information, and this is what followed in the wake of the unpredictable and deadly Covid-19. But what does it mean for the journalists responsible for gathering such information and relaying it? It means bidding farewell to set work hours or weekends and immersing oneself in the situation, to be able to give people accurate and verified facts and updates. During such crises, their role expands to also anticipating further questions and seeking answers for them in good time.

In India, when the entire nation went into lockdown in March 2020, businesses switched to remote work; trains and flights came to a complete halt; and shops shut down—but journalists and media professionals continued doing their job, having been categorised as "essential workers". They were required to operate at double the efficiency than before. From understanding the nature of the virus to its medical hazards to the economic impact and the on-ground reality, the task was to collate as much relevant and vetted information for the masses as possible.

But in the midst of a pandemic that does not discriminate, it is hard to segregate the personal and professional. How does one explain to a six-year-old kid to not touch his mother? How does one battle the frustration of loneliness? How does one give up the fear of a loved one getting infected? The families of essential workers had no choice but to live with this constant fear hovering over them.

Soon after Covid-19 was declared a pandemic, news media outlets rapidly saw record levels of engagement as audiences increasingly wanted information about the rapidly changing situation. Thomson Reuters Foundation accurately observes that "the pandemic has offered an opportunity to embrace new tools, skills and storytelling techniques".

The World Association of Newspapers and News Publishers found that various media outlets launched coronavirus-themed podcasts, alerts and newsletters designed to cater to this demand. Infographics and explainer videos became highly popular, with both traditional and non-traditional news outlets producing such content. As journalism.co.uk says, "These efforts reflect the ability of journalists to creatively communicate vital public health messages and meet audiences where they are."

As Covid-19 became the all-consuming interest of the nation, news channels adapted quickly. In their capacity as citizens, journalists had to adhere to the rules of safety; as a crucial source of critical and relevant information, they had to obtain accurate facts and relay them to audiences as efficiently as possible. During the first wave, news content focused largely on the virus itself—a novel and poorly understood threat—and new information as it came in. Journalists also communicated lockdown information, policy and protocol updates, and safety measures.

With the onslaught of the second wave, the focus shifted, especially in India. Even as the virus had become a familiar menace, there were more pressing associated issues—a collapsing medical infrastructure; lack of beds, oxygen cylinders and important drugs; and updates on vaccine rollout. Journalists were reporting live on the availability, or lack thereof, of beds and other life-saving equipment for Covid-19 patients. Some media houses started their own resource initiatives, going above and beyond their roles as journalists. NDTV, for instance, started a plasma donation drive.

At the same time, however, journalists and media channels had to deal with a growing censorship from the government and other authorities. Facebook, Instagram and Twitter were asked to remove posts about the health crisis. Medianama, an online news portal, reported that the authorities had requested the censorship of posts by journalists on social media sites on the grounds that this was necessary to prevent the spread of rumours. As noted in a study conducted by Thomson Reuters Foundation, in addition to the internal pressures on journalism to adapt and evolve, Covid-19 has reinforced external pressures in the form of attacks on journalists, and new laws that limit press freedom, which can jeopardise lives by limiting reporting, debates and discussions about the pandemic and the ways to tackle it.

When the second wave of Covid-19 hit India in 2021, journalists were once again tasked with the responsibility of keeping the public informed and assured. This time, as the virus spread faster, wider and claimed more lives, news personnel found themselves in a far more precarious situation. Yet, despite constantly being on the field and on duty, in Covid-19 wards and crematoriums, putting their lives at risk, journalists have not been considered as frontline workers and did not receive priority during the vaccination drives.

In a study conducted jointly by the International Centre for Journalists and the Tow Centre for Digital Journalism at Columbia University, involving 1,406 participants across 125 countries,

70 per cent of the respondents rated the psychological toll as their biggest challenge during the pandemic. Over 80 per cent noted at least one negative psychological effect—anxiety, burnout, difficulty sleeping and a sense of helplessness. According to a study quoted in India Today, *over 300 media persons, including many well-known journalists, lost their lives due to the virus. "On average, three journalists died every day in April 2021 and this number increased to four in May." A report by the Institute of Perception Studies states 238 verified journalist deaths due to Covid-19 from April 2020 to May 2021, with the second wave claiming nearly double the lives compared to the first one.*

In the face of such perils and without the same infrastructural support that other frontline workers have received, field reporters continue to risk their mental and physical well-being for the greater public good of disseminating accurate news and information about the ongoing crisis.

Surbhi R. Sharma has been a journalist for over eighteen years, but has never witnessed a crisis similar to Covid-19. From conquering the challenges posed by her profession to doing justice to her role as a mother, wife and daughter-in-law, Surbhi narrates what it has been like to report during a pandemic. She takes us through the psychological battles of the process, and how to deal with reality when your biggest fear eventually comes true.

*

Let's wind the clock back to the beginning of 2020.

Coronavirus—now one of the most frequently used words by all of us, then only the name of a new and unfamiliar disease originating in China. Journalists, given the very nature of our profession, were the first of common citizens to be allowed access to the details of the disease: the pace of spread, the number of casualties, etc. For me, the most pertinent question was: *How is India—a country where addressing healthcare issues is often relegated to the bottom of the to-do list of priorities—going to deal with this?*

I soon realised that everybody was asking the same question, and nobody seemed to know the answer.

Even as Covid-19 was taking over the world, India had its energies and efforts focused on another national issue—the Ram Mandir. The Ayodhya dispute has been a 492-year-long battle of religious ideologies, land and faith. On 9 November 2019, the battle came to a legal end when the Supreme Court of India finally announced its verdict and ordered the creation of a trust to build the Ram Mandir. In April 2020, when it was time for the temple to take physical form, my team decided to travel to Ayodhya to shoot a few special episodes.

17 March 2020

I woke up to the news of Covid-19 cases increasing rapidly in states like Maharashtra and Bihar. The rate at which this virus was spreading had become a cause for serious concern, to say the least. Regardless, I had a flight to catch, so I packed my stuff and left for the airport.

Landing in Lucknow, I got off the plane, got inside a car and drove for three straight hours to find myself finally standing on one of the world's most historic lands—Ayodhya, or as locals call it, Ram Janmabhoomi, the birthplace of Lord Ram.

Here, Covid-19 seemed to exist only in whispers, no trace of masks, no smell of sanitiser in the air … not much concern at all. For the people of Ayodhya, the sole spectacle was watching their temple finally take shape, one brick at a time. The anticipation was palpable. We prepared ourselves to cover this national interest story; everything was in place, ready to go. Our schedule was planned by the office in such a manner that we had to shoot three shows in two days, get back to Delhi and revisit Ayodhya on 26 March to shoot the Bhumi Pujan. March 17–19 went exactly as planned.

On my way back to Delhi, I had a word with my boss about the plan of action ahead. Considering that Covid-19 cases were rising, I wasn't sure if going home would be the best option. "What do you want to do?" my boss asked. I had two options. I could go home, but that would mean putting at risk my seven-year-old boy, my husband and my mother-in-law. Alternatively, I could check into a hotel next to my house in Delhi and quarantine there.

The one hour went by in a jiffy, and I landed in Delhi. The Indira Gandhi International Airport had a total of around fifty people. I counted in disbelief. One of the world's busiest airports was shutting down. Shopkeepers were in a rush, pulling their shutters and leaving for good. I asked, "*Bhaiya yahan kya chal raha hai?* (What's going on here?)" He replied, "*Madam, sab band ho raha hai; poora desh band ho raha hai. Hum ja rahe hain.* (Everything is shutting down; the whole country is shutting down. We are leaving.)"

It was at that moment that I knew. Whatever was about to unfold would be marked in the annals of history.

Even though a formal lockdown hadn't been announced yet, you could see all actions prophesying it. *How will we resume our show if things don't get better? Does that even matter right now?* Caught in this riot of anxious thoughts, the rational journalist gave way to the vulnerable mother, and I broke down. Looking back, I think it was the national panic turning into helplessness and hopelessness! The sinking feeling when you lose your grip or aren't the one in control—of how you function, how others around you function, how things *should* function. I had no answers, only questions. How was I supposed to pull myself together and be strong?

I then found myself a taxi and headed to a hotel, around 10 kilometres from my house, to quarantine. "Quarantine" essentially means putting people who have arrived from elsewhere or been potentially exposed to an infectious disease in a particular place for a specific period of time, usually the duration that is considered the average incubation period of the particular disease. For Covid-19, it was fourteen days.

My husband brought over clothes, essentials and toiletries that I'd be needing for the next two weeks. He dropped off the duffel bag at the hotel reception, having been sprayed multiple times with a sanitiser. I stood six feet away from him, and we exchanged longing looks. I gave him a reassuring smile, trying to say, *I'm fine, you don't have to worry.* He returned my smile with one that reassured me that he'd take care of himself, our son and my mother-in-law. The whole act of exchanging bags was a funny one because it felt like we were sneakily exchanging some sort of explosives or drugs.

22 March 2020

The inkling I got at the airport on 19 March 2020 materialised on 22 March 2020 when Prime Minister Narendra Modi declared a Janata Curfew—a day-long nationwide lockdown in response to the pandemic, to implement social distancing within the population and slow down the spread of the virus.

Sitting in my hotel room, I stared out the window ... what a sight it was! Not a single soul on the streets—no car, no cycle, no pedestrian even. I'd never seen anything like this before. On a regular day, Delhi, the national capital of India would be bustling with activity and car honks. On that day, if you had stepped outside, you would have only heard the rhythm of your breath. All of India stayed indoors, looking out through windows, finding the same sight everywhere.

I went back to my bed. With a piece of paper, a pen and lots of time at hand, I began sketching. It was an attempt to fast-forward time or stay oblivious to each passing second. That evening, my hotel room phone rang. "Ma'am, when can you check out? There are talks that a nationwide lockdown will soon be announced, so we've been asked to shut down the hotel immediately." I took a second to make sense of what he was saying. *Was he serious?* The moment I uttered the words, I realised that there was not much scope to *not be serious*. Yes, I was literally being thrown out of the hotel I was supposed to be quarantining in. With no solution at hand, I decided to return home and isolate myself in one room.

The moment I walked in, my seven-year-old ran towards me but I could not even hug him. I had to explain to him that he couldn't touch or hug me for another ten days as I was still under quarantine. Disappointed, we both patiently waited for ten days to go by and finally once my isolation period ended, I ran towards my son, picked him up and hugged him for as long as I could, content that he was safe and sound in my arms. If someone had told me then that this would be the last time I would be able to hug him for the next six months, I might have held on for longer.

After that day, everything changed. As expected, a nationwide lockdown was announced by the prime minister on 24 March 2020.

"*Aaj raat 12 baje se, sampoorn desh mein, sampoorn lockdown hone jaa raha hai.* (From 12 tonight, there will be a complete lockdown all over India)," he declared.

And that was it: a whole nation was under lockdown, for twenty-one days.

This move was somewhat anticipated. Elsewhere in the world, countries that were failing to control the growing Covid-19 cases, like Spain and Italy, had also declared nationwide lockdowns at this point. Yet, it was still a bit hard to digest now that it had actually happened.

My way of working changed, from shooting lives from the terrace of my hotel to finding ways to function despite the restrictions ... life had suddenly become enormously exhausting. Our responsibilities increased manifold, involving reporting from Covid-19 wards to cemeteries to interacting with hospital staff to attendants to the frontline warriors. Of course, this is in addition to regular day-to-day news operations.

As a silver lining, digital media, which had already been on the rise over the last decade, received an extra boost as a direct result of the pandemic. Covid-19 bolstered the speed of both adoption and application in all industry segments, and this included the news industry as well. The move online was well-sustained, too, with mobile devices in every hand, the easy availability of high-speed data, and the freedom of consumption not bound by time. Moreover, the rapid growth of digital news mediums, a time when layoffs were rampant and the economy badly impacted, gave a great career opportunity to those in the unorganised sector. Independent journalists who were doing good work started gaining traction and earning a livelihood, without being dependent on formal employment. Even for established news organisations like ours, the digital landscape became important and offered a great platform to generate incremental revenues, be future ready, and engage and stay connected to our viewers and critics.

At the office, when we did go there, things had changed dramatically. We were (and are still) required to engage in a strictly Covid-19-appropriate behaviour—masking, sanitising, maintaining safe distance. The newsrooms are a large unit and are treated as a social bubble. A single infection inside a newsroom could not only risk the health of many others but potentially threaten the entire news operation—as it happened with cricketers during the 2021 Indian Premier League (IPL). In all of this, my organisation, India TV, was heart-warmingly supportive and quick to action. They took a humanitarian approach from the get-go, investing heavily on the safety of all employees. Mask supplies, regular sanitisations through the day, sanitisation tunnels, temperature checks, careful shift assignments, work from home for all staff who weren't required for daily operations of news broadcast, medical-aid provisions, facilitating fully funded quarantines at hotels for suspected staff members with limited resources at home, conducting regular check-ups and tests ... These are just a few steps that were taken as an immediate response to the outbreak.

Despite being relatively better informed due to my profession, the months from April to July 2020 tested every fibre of my being—as a person, as a journalist, as a wife, as a mother. Every morning, the bulletin news got a tad darker. "Today, 500 people died due to the novel coronavirus", "Today, India recorded 80,000 cases, the highest reported in one day than any other country", "Today, 65 health workers have succumbed to the virus". It came to a point where I found myself becoming more and more robotic in the way I operated. I became immune to hearing and reporting such devastating news. What was happening to me? We were living through a global pandemic, and I was getting tired.

That my shifts had become erratic didn't help. I'd leave home at 2 p.m. and spend hours in the newsroom, which had effectively become a Covid-19 echo chamber. I'd return home late into the night at around 1 a.m., disinfect myself and take a shower. To be extra careful, I would meet family members only nine hours after I'd showered. This drill went on for days on end.

In all of this, what I found the hardest was answering my son's innocent questions. Both his parents were media professionals, which needed them to be on the field most of the time, while his friends' parents were almost always home due to the lockdown. He'd ask, "*Mumma, aap aur papa hi kyun kaam pe jaate ho jab Ritesh ke mummy papa saara din uske saath rehete hain? Kya mein aapke saath ek din mein sirf 2 hi ghante spend kar sakta hun? Mumma, mein aapko kab hug karke so paunga?* (Why do only you and dad have to go for work when Ritesh's parents are home with him all day? Am I allowed to spend only two hours of the day with you? Mom, when can I next hug you and sleep?)"

Each day, I saw him get his hopes up only to be disappointed. I couldn't let this go on. Something had to be done to change this negativity that was affecting all of us. It had been five months, and we hadn't managed to spend any quality time together. Finally, my husband and I decided to change our perspective on the situation and we came up with some ground rules.

1. No one in the house would utter the word or talk about coronavirus for a whole month.
2. We would spend more time with each other and try to recreate indoors the things we'd do outdoors.
3. We would find creative outlets for our feelings or experiences, whether positive or negative.

4. We would stay away from news and social media.

With these rules in place, the atmosphere in the house took a 180-degree turn. We found it easier to avoid sulking or complaining, and the feelings of disappointment dissipated. We'd wake up early every morning, have breakfast together, play hopscotch for several hours in our little living room, and spend time talking to each other. We carved out extra time from our busy schedules to accommodate these healthy changes. This time allowed me to revive my love for sketching; I'd find moments to sit and doodle away. I had finally found an escape from the mounting dread of the situation outside. I felt all right, and a sense of normalcy was restored, at least in a psychological sense.

As the cliché rightly goes, *nothing lasts forever*. On 19 August 2020, my husband started feeling sick and complained of a headache. The same week, two people from his department at office tested positive for Covid-19. As per the protocols, my husband got tested as well, along with me, my son and my mother-in-law. We gave our swabs and returned home, anxiously waiting for the results to come the following morning. That night, my son said, "Mumma, I can't wait for the test results to come quickly. It will be negative, and *phir dekhna mein aapko ek badi jhappi de kar sounga.* (you will see that I will hug you tightly and sleep)."

The next day, results came. My husband, my little boy, my mother-in-law were all positive. To my utter shock, I tested negative. For the first couple of hours, I was in denial. I called up the lab to crosscheck my son's result two or three times.

How could this happen?

Almost on cue, my mind spiralled into the darkest recesses and brought me back to exactly where I was in the initial days of the pandemic. The overthinking, the panicking, the "questioning everything" … all over again. What I'd feared the most during these months had finally happened. I had three Covid-19 positive family members living under the same roof. *What now?* From being locked inside a house, we went into being locked inside rooms. I was in one room, and the other three in another room together. Days bled into each other; weeks felt erratic—some went by fast, some painfully slow. There was an uneasy calm where no one could do anything except *wait*. Waiting for the wait to end. It was no longer about loving or hating the virus—that made no difference. The words *jispe beeti hai, ussi ko pata hai ki uspar kya beeti hai* (only the one who's gone through something will know what it feels like) echoed in my mind. So often, I come across these quotes and sayings about the fragility of life, about the transience of things, about change being the only constant. The pandemic, and my personal brush with it, brought those ideas to life in a very literal sense.

After a while, the shadow passed. To my greatest fortune, everyone in our family suffered only moderate symptoms. While it was a harrowing experience, it gave me a better, fuller understanding of the crisis and the significance of my role as a journalist. I feel more in sync with the suffering the deadly virus has brought us and more equipped to take-up and raise the issues critical to fighting this menace. I am proud to be part of a fraternity that has always been at the epicentre of everything that impacts us as a society, nation or as the citizens of the planet earth. We have doled out news from wars, to terror attacks. We are now doing the same from Covid-19 wards. Indeed, this profession is not for the weak-hearted.

In light of the second wave, the reality seemed even more uncertain than it did the last time. I don't know what happens after this, when life will return to *normal*—if it ever will. But I know one thing (and this applies to all precarious situations in life): We are stronger than we think we are. There is a lot we feel incapable of handling, but we cannot predict how we would react in a situation until we have been thrown into it. The real test lies in navigating through it and knowing that we possess the ability to overcome it.

Did I think I was confident of handling everything that happened? Absolutely not.

Am I still surviving and managing? Somehow, *yes.*

20

A Race against Time

Sunash B. Sharma, Covid-19 Human Challenge Trial Volunteer

Editors' Note

During a worldwide outbreak of a disease, the primary concern is to prevent infection. However, there are hundreds of individuals who volunteer to get infected, keeping in mind the larger good that can come from it. Developing a Covid-19 vaccine had been the need of the hour since the coronavirus pandemic broke out.

Apart from the scientists and experts who tirelessly work with the technicalities of producing a vaccine, a range of other factors also play an equally important role in the process. The human challenge trial, which calls for volunteers willing to have the vaccine tested on them, is one such factor and Sunash B. Sharma is one such volunteer.

The coronavirus vaccine trials require large numbers of volunteers, primarily for researchers to be able to look for any and all rare side effects. "The initial trials involve tens or maybe hundreds of people, and there are sometimes side effects that only show up when you look at a lot of people," shared NPR science correspondent Joe Palca, "but the other thing is you need to make sure people get exposed. And this is where things get really interesting because researchers can't go out and tell people, yes, now if we've given you a shot, go see if you can get exposed to the virus. That would be unethical." Over 1,00,000 people in the UK are taking part in coronavirus vaccine trials. Almost half a million Americans signed up to participate in Covid-19 vaccine clinical trials, but in order for the trials to be completed, researchers still needed more than 1 million additional people to volunteer. Bharat Biotech successfully recruited 23,000 volunteers.

Sunash is among the hundreds of people who have signed up to participate in the human challenge trials. A volunteer is made well aware of the risk to life that come with developing an effective vaccine fast. A large discourse around such a trial in the US concerns ethics. Infecting a young, healthy body with a life-threatening virus defies the principles of morals and hence, is a point of debate that is deferring the process of starting the trials. However, at the end of the day, the ultimate choice lies with people like Sunash who, at the age of twenty-three, have taken the decision to participate.

Sunash B. Sharma has completed his graduation in Applied Physics and Computer Science from California Institute of Technology. He is curious about all things research and impact. His story aims to take us through the psychological as well as the technical consequences of such a decision. In addition to the processes involved in a challenge trial like this, we are made privy to the phases of vaccine development and the obstacles that it poses.

*

We know viruses like Covid-19 have few widely used treatments and no known cure. This puts everyone including citizens, medical experts and scientists across the world in a largely uncharted territory. However, a hotly contested strategy of deliberate exposure (that I've recently learned about), known as a human challenge trial, is said to speed up the process of identifying effective coronavirus vaccines. An immediate question is: Why would someone participate in one of these trials? What motivates them? Possible immunity? Financial compensation? Or just the opportunity to help science or be a part of history? I was keen on exploring answers to these questions. My story is centred around this and more.

Human challenge trials deliberately expose participants to infection, in order to study diseases and test vaccines or treatments. In the aftermath of the Covid-19 crisis, thousands have volunteered to willingly get infected with the virus to contribute to the vaccination development process.

I am one of them.

At this point, it is not a question of whether I should do this or not. *I am doing it.* I view it as something I *must* do. I'm relatively young and healthy and if I were to get infected by Covid-19, my odds of fighting it would be relatively high. When I see the burden this pandemic has placed on human life around me, the cost I might have to pay seems almost negligible. The number of people succumbing to the virus every day is unbelievable. Each passing minute, this number increases. Of course, I understand that my volunteering alone won't have a huge impact on the development of the vaccine, but even if I can help it develop sooner by a day, week or month … that would still save a lot of lives—a significant contribution.

One of the common questions I get asked is, "Where did you find the courage to do this? How can you willingly risk your life?" Honestly, the answer is rather mundane. I learned of human challenge trials from a story aired by a news channel that triggered within me the thought of volunteering. We'd all been sitting at home, having lost any sense of control over our life, actions, behaviours or routines. Watching that ad restored a sense of control in me. Almost instantly, I knew I wanted to contribute.

I could do something.

I could contribute towards controlling the chaos in a minuscule yet important manner.

I signed up through an initiative called 1daysooner.org that advocates for people who want to participate in high-impact medical trials, including Covid-19 challenge trials. Their vision propagates a manner through which a volunteer is fully informed regarding the process, its pros and cons, side-effects, the ethical measures, etc. The first step was simply to fill a form on the website. It wasn't a terribly difficult decision to sign up, as not only was I really motivated to do it from a moral perspective but also signing up in and of itself is not a commitment to become a volunteer; there's a whole other process of volunteer selection and screening, at any point during which I could have opted out. I interacted with the communications director a bit, at least three or four times during the process.

Subconsciously, I had already made up my mind. But to better evaluate my decision, I began researching rigorously about the pros and cons, the long-term impacts, and the logistics involved. One might assume that my fear would revolve around the risks involved and the probability of death. But that wasn't it. In fact, the risk of dying from the virus is one in 10,000 if you are below the age of thirty-four. To put this in perspective, the risk of death from a kidney donation is one in 3,300. What struck me more was the sheer lack of understanding about the long-term effects of Covid-19. The virus can cause permanent damage to one's lungs as well as kidneys. They are known to create grey patches in the lungs, which may never heal despite recovery from the virus. It was information like this that really weighed on me.

Regardless, after reading up a lot on the subject and running a cost–benefit analysis, I realised that the benefits of volunteering far outweighed the risks. I was convinced. But the bigger task was getting my parents on board. How do you convince your parents to give you the permission to risk your life? Initially, I decided to spare them the worry by not telling them. Rationality doesn't take the forefront when it comes to family; emotion becomes the predominant language. However, when I began to give interviews expressing my thoughts on human challenge trials, they knew.

To my surprise, my dad has been quite supportive. He is proud of what I'm doing, even though he questions himself, wondering if he's failing in his duties as a parent by letting me participate in the challenge trials. However, parents proudly send their children off to war all the time, and this pandemic is a war in many ways—against disease, against hopelessness. A war in which victory will help everyone on the planet. In essence, even though my father feels conflicted, his feelings of pride have overcome his fear for me.

My mother, on the other hand, has been fairly opposed to my participation. Who can blame her? She, too, is proud of my sensibilities and respects where I'm coming from, but she is unable to come to terms with the reality of signing up for such a risk. I understand her predicament. If, instead of me, my child was signing up for such a trial, I couldn't say the decision would be easy for me. She knows that I am an adult who must make my own choices in life. At the same time, she wants to have more detailed discussions about the long-term effects of being infected with the virus. She will support my final decision whether she personally agrees with it or not.

The process of developing a vaccine is quite elaborate and I was curious to find out how a medicine for such a large-scale catastrophe is developed. There's too much at stake to mess it up. So, I started with understanding the basics of what happens behind the scenes before one gets jabbed.

There are four phases involved in the development of a vaccine, and each takes a substantial amount of time. Phase 1 of vaccine development involves figuring out purely whether a new vaccine candidate is safe and if it generates the expected immune response. Phase 2 involves figuring out the correct vaccine dosage and expanding to a larger pool of volunteers to further evaluate the safety and immune response. After phase 2, there are two options, which may even be done concurrently: a phase 3 vaccine trial or a human challenge trial.

In a phase 3 trial, a large number of volunteers are given either the vaccine or a placebo, then let out into the world to see if the real vaccine decreases chances of getting infected with the virus compared to the placebo. A human challenge trial uses a smaller sample size of healthy volunteers, administers half of them a vaccine and half a placebo, and then directly infects all volunteers with Covid-19. This is where challenge trials become a double-edged sword, posing an advantage but also a risk. Instead of waiting for a small portion of phase 3 volunteers to be randomly infected with Covid-19 through interaction with the rest of the world, a challenge trial directly infects all volunteers, decreasing the timescale on which a potential vaccine is evaluated. This allows access to data about how the vaccine interacts with the virus.

In addition, the human challenge trial requires a preparation of what is known as a "challenge dose". This dosage, injected into a volunteer, has a lesser viral load where the symptoms experienced aren't severe. The sample size for this stage is relatively less, somewhere between twenty to eighty people. Once the challenge dose is injected, scientists evaluate the safety of the vaccine and measure the immune response that it generates after monitoring the volunteers in quarantine facilities. Depending on the symptoms the volunteers show or don't show, the results are evaluated, and the effectiveness of the vaccine is further assessed.

But the crucial challenge when it comes to Covid-19 is achieving the desired result in a much shorter time period than usual. A recent study in the National Bureau of Economic Research found that accelerating the development of a vaccine by just one month would save 8,000 lives in the US alone.

The time crunch calls for a much larger sample size, extremely precise monitoring of responses, and almost a negligible margin for error. Once the responses are analysed with certainty and the vaccine is ready, the trial enters its last phase: regulatory approval and licensure process. At this stage, vaccine manufacturers submit an application to regulatory bodies for the review of the clinical trial data to ascertain whether the vaccine is safe and effective. Thereafter, the manufacturing and distribution finally takes place, making the vaccine accessible to the world.

Once I had decided on volunteering for the trial, impatience set in. The whole process takes a frustrating amount of time. One of the main barriers to conducting challenge trails in the US concerns the ethics of it. This delays decision making and, in turn, the rolling out of the trial. On the one hand, it is considered unethical to deliberately infect young and healthy people with a virus that has no cure. Even if the chance of death is minimal, a challenge trial may severely damage parts of a volunteer's body or its functioning in the long term. However, at the same time, if the challenge trials are successful, they could significantly reduce the time taken to build and distribute a vaccine, which would end up saving several lives. The trade-off is significant. From a volunteer's point of view, several factors need to be considered, such as compensation—for lost time, opportunities and, potentially, life. In light of this, it is important to remember that in a trial like this, volunteers will likely be given monetary compensation, but how much is the question. It is important to take into account whether the compensation is enough for what is at stake and what is being lost in the process. You are made aware of all the risks in a transparent manner. There is an upfront communication with no room for loopholes. At the end of the day, it is your call.

In simple words, the aim is to make a Covid-19 vaccine available globally within a year, while vaccines usually take over five years to develop. I could help speed up the process. But I could also be inviting long-term damages and there is always that 0.01 per cent chance of death. Do I go ahead with it? *I must.*

In December 2020, the first shot of Covid-19 vaccine was received by a woman in the US. This news was the first good one in what felt like years. It was a relief to finally know that there was a solution. The vaccine is not just an essential weapon in preventing the virus itself but it also prevents severe illness and death in case of infection post vaccination. Since experts and medical authorities are in the process of learning from the responses of the vaccines, they are ascertaining the effectiveness of the vaccines against different variants of the virus.

Now that the vaccine is here, I'm happy about my decision to have volunteered, as I feel that my volunteering may have indirectly contributed to the awareness of such human challenge trials (for future pandemics) and potentially trust of the vaccine/science in general. For example, the UK is now doing a Covid-19 reinfection study that was motivated in part by the idea of a human challenge trial. I'm also happy that several vaccines are working around the world. But with all that, I do have a sense of sadness. It took around nine months from the pandemic starting to the first vaccine being administered in the US. With a quickly approved challenge trial, that time may have been cut significantly, starting the vaccination campaign months earlier, avoiding thousands of deaths, lots of economic strain, perhaps even avoiding some of the new variants spreading (if herd immunity were established before they developed).

I'm not surprised about the degree to which people are questioning vaccines (at least in the US). I'm not sure how much challenge trials would have helped on that front, but with all the misinformation spread during the pandemic, some hesitancy around the vaccine is understandable. While I'm all for human challenge trials, I do think developing a vaccine that fast might even worsen people's perception of the vaccine's safety. But that would be far outweighed by the lives saved by getting those who are vulnerable vaccinated sooner.

Yes, we have the key to ending this pandemic with the vaccines, even if it took a long time to get them. At this point, it's a matter of getting as many people immunized as possible while curtailing the virus spread, which seems much more tractable than a pandemic with no end in sight. I'm also hopeful that the next pandemic will be far less disruptive given the lessons our society has learned about this one.

Epilogue: Grappling with the Second Wave

16 March 2021

A New Normal?

Hope and reality are pointing towards a less mundane, recuperative 2021. Of course, with the necessary safety protocols, cafes are up and running, offices are operational with 50 per cent capacity and Covid-19 is now an omnipresent reality. Not a threat. Days where no new infections are being reported are relieving. The nation has now moved onto the next spectacle: State assembly elections 2021.

This year will decide the fate of West Bengal, Assam, Kerala, Tamil Nadu and Puducherry. As a result, politicians and the media are investing all their energies on the elections. Door-to-door campaigns, roadshows, rallies, you name it. But amidst this political orgasm, social distancing, wearing a mask, avoiding physical contact almost seems like a joke.

In some ways, it's a relief to even imagine a post-Covid-19 world. Any idea of normalcy being restored instils hope. The idea of being able to meet friends, family who live across the country is so exciting. We also haven't taken a vacation in a year! The thrill of packing a suitcase full of beach clothes, of clicking images without a mask covering half the face, or of simply feeling the airplane take off: it's definitely something we miss. As unexpected as it may be, some of us even miss going to an office, clocking in at 10 a.m., clocking out at 7 p.m. and doing it all over again the next day. A sense of routine would be therapeutic.

28 March 2021

The Calm before the Storm

Today, Maharashtra imposed a night curfew, allowing no gatherings of more than five people between 8 p.m. and 7 a.m. This is to extend until 15 April 2021. Weekends will see complete shutdowns which means that shops dealing with non-essential goods and services, malls, restaurants and theatres will all remain shut.

It is the first time this year that any kind of restrictions due to Covid-19 have been imposed. The curfew comes after Maharashtra recorded 25,883 cases of Covid-19 in a single day earlier in March. It is the highest one-day spike in cases since the pandemic began in our country.

11 April 2021

The Second Wave

India's Covid-19 graph trajectory is worrisome. Some say that the number of average daily cases being recorded now has overtaken the peak witnessed in September 2020. News channels and social media are both echoing a possible catastrophe. They're calling it the second wave of the novel coronavirus.

19 April 2021

Déjà Vu

New Delhi, our place of residence, is witnessing a week-long lockdown, starting today till 26 April. Government officers, diplomatic staff, medical staff, travellers and medical patients, those who are going to get inoculated are allowed movement. To be honest, this feels exactly like a repeat of 2020. Only, much worse.

This time it feels more real, close and inescapable. Every household around us has a Covid-19 positive patient. The virus is present in our immediate families. Celebrities and politicians are succumbing to the virus.

Life was finally starting to take a positive turn, we'd just got a grip on work, and were regaining the sense of safety we'd lost last year. However, this sets us back emotionally. The year started out on a positive note, but the way it's shaping up to be is upsetting. This feels like the world's worst hangover.

21 April 2021

B.1.617

The current wave of Covid-19 has a different clinical behaviour. It's affecting young adults. It's affecting families. It's a new thing altogether. Two-month-old babies are getting infected.

India has a homegrown variant called B.1.617, which some in the news media and medical industry have concluded is responsible for the ferocious second wave. While it's almost certainly true B.1.617 is playing a role, it's unclear how much it is contributing directly to the surge. Researchers say other factors could lead to more infections among young people, such as India's schools, which had started reopening in recent months after the country's first wave.

The variant in India is sometimes called "the double mutant", though the name is a misnomer because it has many more mutations than two. Scientists say that different variants seem to dominate specific parts of India. For instance, the B.1.617 variant has been detected in a large number of samples from Maharashtra. By contrast, the B.1.1.7 variant is rising quickly in New Delhi.

25 April 2021

The Oxygen Crisis

It's on social media, it's in the messages we receive from people, it's on the news: India is struggling to breathe. There is a severe shortage of medical oxygen in India and hospitals are sending SOS messages to the government warning them that they have only a few hours of oxygen supply left. Instances of patients dying due to lack of oxygen are making headlines. It's come to a point where going to hospitals is no longer an option. People are resorting to doing whatever they can to take care of a Covid-19 patient at home. Many stand outside oxygen supplier's shops for hours to refill or buy new cylinders. How did we get here? We were just starting to find our footing but now India is sinking. This is a nightmare.

As families of the sick fill social media with pleas for oxygen and cremation grounds burn thousands of bodies daily, India has gone from declaring victory over Covid-19 to suffering its gravest emergency in decades. My twenty-four-year-old cousin was rushed to the hospital when his oxygen levels began to drop. This young life, beaming with energy, came to an end ten days later, when the hospital ran out of necessary medication required to save his life. My family is still grieving the loss.

Some days are spent simply amplifying requests for plasma donors or oxygen cylinders or hospital beds. Seated in one position, typing rapidly on the phone, making phone calls to all imaginable friends, acquaintances, hospital owners, doctors, just to find one verified lead. It is difficult to think of any other aspect of life. It takes a kind of mental toll on you, one that you cannot express.

There is no one reason for why this is happening. We're all to blame but there is no one to hold accountable. Somewhere, we as a country let our guards down too soon against a raging virus. Complacency? Perhaps. There are still people who refuse to wear masks and frown upon the need to practise social distancing. Muddled administrative measures transformed India's successful battle against Covid-19 to it being one of the worst-hit countries in the world. Despite the gravity of the situation, watching Indian politicians hold big election rallies is unbelievable. Some news outlets have said that the roots of India's crisis lie in the previous one. While the first wave had a terrible hit on the country, it was an understatement to what we are experiencing today. Many industry leaders and top government officials were acting as though the problem had been resolved.

But as many comparisons between the first and second wave surface, here's a clear difference in the nature of the second wave (so far):

1. Higher rate of infection: Due to the various mutations of the virus itself, more people are getting infected and that too, at a much faster pace.
2. Young population, equally susceptible: While people over sixty were highest at risk during the first wave, things now seem bleak for even the younger generation. The chief minister of Delhi, Arvind Kejriwal, said that

45 per cent of the patients in Delhi were below forty-five years old.

3. Changes in symptoms: Unlike the usual fever, sore throat, dry cough and cold, this time around the symptoms for Covid-19 have also seen a slight shift. The new strains of the virus are aggressive on the vital organs and cause more symptoms. These now include nausea, vomiting as well as acute abdominal pain.
4. Trouble detecting the virus: The RT-PCR test that is considered the most reliable test for Covid-19 has raised concerns. There have been instances where patients with typical symptoms of Covid-19 end up testing negative despite multiple RT-PCR tests. Some attribute this trend to the fact that the new variants of Covid-19 settle deep into the lungs, which makes it difficult to detect them. Doctors now say that they cannot completely rely on RT PCR tests alone.

29 April 2021

As of today, the country and its 1.4 billion lives continue to battle the coronavirus. We live at one of the epicentres of the second wave. The country's capital suffers as hospitals survive on limited hours of oxygen supply. We hear news of close friends, family members and acquaintances experiencing the demise of their loved ones, almost every day. Compared to 2020, we see the fear of death and infection increase manifold. Each day, India sets a new record of Covid-19 cases and deaths. This soaring mortality rate means that cremation grounds ran out of space to bury the dead. People are having to resort to bidding farewell to their loved ones inside a parking lot or a makeshift pyre on a footpath. Students are witnessing cancelled examinations, virtual classes and a severe lack of jobs.

1 May 2021

A New Global Record

The situation is frightening. India is recording more infections per day than any other since the pandemic began. For many, across the country, including some of our closest family members, the pain has been accompanied by a realisation of their worst fear: when the people we love need us the most, we can't be there to help.

What was most horrifying for us and citizens across the country was when India reported 4,01,993 new cases of the coronavirus in a day. This was a global record. Ever since the second wave came knocking at our doors, India has pushed the world record for daily new cases higher and higher, while averaging over 3,000 Covid-19 deaths each day, with more than 2,00,000 dead in total. And evidence suggests the official numbers vastly understate the toll.

To say that we are constantly petrified is an understatement. We have come to equate the word luxury with: availability of oxygen, access to a bed in hospitals, and not having lost a loved one. It feels as though we are acting out the plot of a zombie apocalypse movie.

Through news reports and research articles, we learnt today that while India is a global power in vaccine production, the country didn't purchase enough doses to protect itself. When the count was relatively low, it exported more than 60 million shots; now exports have essentially been shut down. The chief executive of Serum Institute of India, the world's largest vaccine manufacturer, is in Britain, having come under increasingly intense pressure at home. He informed a few news outlets that he had been receiving threatening phone calls from business tycoons, industrialists and other influential people in India to expedite the supply of the vaccine. "Threats is an understatement," Poonawalla said. "The level of expectation and aggression is really unprecedented … I'm staying here for an extended time, because I don't want to go back to that situation," he added. "Everything falls on my shoulders, but I can't do it alone."

2 May 2021

Vaccine Hesitancy

The goal was to inoculate 300 million people for Covid-19 by August 2021, but the rising cases and deaths lend greater urgency to the drive. India is known as a global pharmaceutical powerhouse. Owing to this reputation, we were all hopeful that the vaccination drive would go smoothly.

India is primarily dependent on two vaccines. One is AstraZeneca's Covishield that is manufactured by the Serum Institute of India. The second is Covaxin, developed by a biotechnological company called Bharat Biotech in collaboration with an Indian government body. With a mild set of controversies surrounding their efficacies and trials, they are currently the main players in India's vaccine strategy.

However, right now, the vaccination drive has been hobbled by bureaucracy, inefficient delivery and a rich–poor disparity. Out of the intended 30 million healthcare and other frontline workers, India has managed to vaccinate only 14 million in its first drive between 16 January and 1 March. We are currently staring at a significant shortage of vaccines.

There's a debate going around worldwide on whether one should get vaccinated or not. Popularly known as "vaccine hesitancy", many find themselves dealing with this hesitancy, including Indians.

The hasty approval of Covaxin for public use before it completed its Phase 3 trials created doubt about the vaccine's safety and efficiency. Several cases of reinfection after vaccination are being reported, adding to people questioning whether they should get vaccinated. This is despite the fact that vaccination would reduce the severity of the disease in the case of reinfection and lowers the rate of transmission.

The second wave of the pandemic is surging through smaller towns, villages and metropolitan cities, and a lockdown is in discussion. The second wave is moving faster than India's bureaucracy. India needs to keep pace.

3 May 2021, 10 a.m.

Vaccine Hesitancy 2.0

In order to be fully vaccinated, experts recommend getting two doses. Over 17.5 million people have received the second dose of the Covid-19 vaccine in India (meaning, they have been completely vaccinated).

Today, a family doctor informed us of some statistics. Approximately 50 per cent of the patients she treats in a day are aged over sixty and have received the first dose of the Covid-19 vaccine; 90 per cent of the patients who visit her clinic or take online consultation have been completely inoculated i.e., received both doses of the Covid-19 vaccine. Still, it is the best hope we have.

3 May 2021, 11:30 p.m.

The Bright Side

It can get overwhelming: a drumbeat of bleak news about the pandemic. Events change so fast that one week seems unrecognizable from the last. Amid the gloom of coronavirus, it's becoming increasingly difficult to find something to feel optimistic about. However, today was spent realising that nothing is all good or all bad. Glimmers of hope exist in every situation, and they are what helps us stay resilient in difficult times.

If we were to crack our heads and think hard about the positives to remember from this situation, these are a few things that come to mind:

a) Kindness is being celebrated: it's not often that acts of fellowship make the headlines. Frontline workers, who have been serving us for decades with unparalleled passion, are finally getting their due credit. We are getting better at being there for each other.

b) Capitalism is momentarily learning to take a back seat: companies, brands and entrepreneurs are trying to be more comfortable with donating 100 per cent of the proceeds to Covid-19 related problems. It's heart-warming to see that philanthropy is winning.

c) Some employers are finally recognising their obligations to their employees: we are witnessing a new kind of understanding and empathy by our bosses. They are asking us to take days off, calling us to check in with us, providing resources to help with mental health issues.

d) It's a daily reminder of exactly how much we can fight against; with a new battle arising every day, humankind has collectively been reaffirmed of its resilience.

e) The vaccines were created at a breakneck speed; there has never been more human ingenuity devoted to a single scientific problem than the one we are facing right now.

13 May 2021, 12:37 p.m.

Another Hurdle

Delhi, along with several other states, was forced to shut down many vaccination centres due to an acute shortage of vaccines.

Worst part? We still don't know if we have hit the peak of this wave yet. As of today, India has fully vaccinated just over 3.82 crore people. While the number may sound large, it is only about 2.8 per cent of a population of about 135 crores.

6 May 2021

Burials: A Public Display and a Lonely Burden

There's something that shakes us up more than the rising number of Covid-19 cases: the way the dead are being buried. Exhausted of Covid-19 relief work, volunteers pick up those who have succumbed to the virus, pile them into ambulances or in the backs of auto-rickshaws that are driven by grieving relatives. It is unbelievable.

At the cremation grounds, the scenes of burials are photographed, filmed and broadcast. They are sent to relatives who couldn't be present at the scene due to lockdown restrictions. It is not unusual to have them displayed in newspapers around the world, and to put India's personal tragedies on display to a global audience. Local residents record the fires on their camera phones, from their roofs or balconies, to show the world why it's imperative to wear masks. One of my acquaintances lost a family member to Covid-19 last month. Only two of the other members were allowed near the body, covered in protective gear. They looked around and saw camerapersons from media companies filming the burial. At that moment, this otherwise intimate ritual seemed to have lost its dignity.

Beyond the images, the cremation grounds bear a painful routine of trauma that will weigh on families long after the headlines fade. In 2021 India, the trauma of loss has become both lonely and public.

15 May 2021

Getting the First Jab!

Today, I got my first dose of the Covid-19 vaccine, Covishield. After two days of constantly refreshing and updating the Co-WIN app, I managed to secure a slot in a vaccination centre. Upon online booking, I was given a list of details including a security code and all other necessary information regarding the timing, venue, date, time of reporting, etc. Many government schools have been converted into vaccination centres and this was one of them. All safety measures and protocols were duly followed in the premises. I entered at 9:45 a.m. and within the first twenty minutes, I was called to get inoculated.

The staff members were extremely kind and helpful. I was told that experiencing side effects such as fever, dizziness and vomiting post vaccination is normal. I was also advised to not consume alcohol for a month and continue to follow safety precautions such as wearing a mask, sanitising and washing hands. I was injected with the Covishield vaccine and the date for my next dose was around three months later, on 7 August 2021. Once people had gotten their jabs, they were asked to spend half an hour in an observatory to ensure that no issues arise post immediate vaccination. In that period, I felt faint and weak for a brief duration but by the end of the half an hour, I was fine.

I just feel extremely grateful to have been able to get myself vaccinated. It is still not entirely accessible to everyone in society, especially those who don't have the digital means to even access the main portal to book their slots. I hope we find a better mechanism that makes this necessity available to all.

14 June 2021

Unlocking 2.0

The Delhi government today announced that it would be lifting most of the lockdown restrictions. Restaurants will be allowed to open at 50 per cent capacity, market complexes and malls will also be open from 10 a.m. to 8 p.m. But schools, colleges, religious gatherings and any form of large get-togethers are still prohibited. But the chief minister warned that these restrictions could be reimposed if cases started to rise again.

After nearly two months, we made plans to meet for lunch at a cafe today. While we were looking forward to stepping outside of our houses, we were very much aware of the precautions we still need to take. Double mask, sanitiser and social distance. It is the new normal and continues to remain so. After all, we still live in a pandemic world.

19 July 2021

Still on Hold

Today is a moment of victory. Well, whatever meaning is left of the word anyway. After three long, draining months, India recorded less than 500 Covid-19 deaths in the last twenty-four hours, reported by the health ministry bulletin. We are returning to some version of normalcy in the capital, but still hearing news about other Indian states facing the crisis again. Maharashtra reported 9,000 new cases. Haryana, Goa and a few other states have announced an extension of the curfew till 26 July. Our friends living in these states share their feelings of continued uncertainty. While the situation in India remains somewhat in control, countries across the world have reported a sudden rise in the number of cases. As reported by *Financial*

Express, the more contagious Delta variant has fuelled a fresh spike in the US and the UK.

As we pen down this diary entry, there is still no light at the end of the tunnel. Covid-19 may not be dominating the news at this very moment but it lingers on in the background—threatening to return, but in which form this time? We don't know. Experts predict that a third wave awaits us. It is expected to peak in October 2021. This surely scares us but seems weirdly inevitable. Earlier, we saw Covid-19 as something that came with an expiration date, something that would eventually end. But now, as unfortunate as it may be, we're gearing up to coexist with it, without knowing when and if this will ever end.

March 2022

Funnily enough, the way we are dealing with the pandemic in a way mirrors our process of writing this book. While we started out with a clear aim to document Covid-19 and its impact on human life, the process of documenting it was based on improvisation. Depending on the situation and uncertain turn of events, our scope expanded, changed and kept progressing. When the second wave hit us, the ability to document that was mere coincidence and a by-product of writing this book in the first place. We initially thought that this book could serve as a reference point for generations to come but once the second wave arrived, we realised that its relevance could also serve the on-going situation.

Every narrator or writer part of this collection whom we interacted with had a central plot around which their pandemic life revolved. Whether it was home-schooling, working from home, losing their job, practising household chores for the first time, or staying away from their family because their job demanded it—everyone had a focal area that defined their experience in the world's longest lockdown. For us, the process of penning these versatile narratives served as that centre.

It defined our approach to the pandemic, especially emotionally. It pushed us to constantly innovate. Learning about accounts such as that of frontline workers, allowed us to be more resilient and grateful. This journey helped in widening our perspective and having a more open-minded outlook towards this experience.

When the world was still grappling with the first wave of coronavirus, we started writing this book with a clear mission: to document stories of unprecedented bravery, innovation and emotion. Today, as we look back on the narrators we interacted with and how they have progressed over the past year, we realise their stories not only matched our expectations but also exceeded them. It is the stories of these twenty narrators and those of the entire world's population that has reminded us of exactly how much strength we carry in us.

We not only accepted that we now live in an unrecognisable world, but also deeply felt every emotion that comes with it. Smoothly, almost instinctively, we transformed every aspect of our day-to-day life. That is a sign of unparalleled optimism. We have also learnt how to channel a similar strength to other personal and professional aspects of life. It's safe to say, we, along with everyone we know, are getting back to square one. Only this time, we are more courageous, more informed and a lot more hopeful.